BIRDS
OF
TORONTO
AND VICINITY

GERALD McKEATING
Illustrated by EWA PLUCIENNIK

LONE
PINE

The Publisher:
Lone Pine Publishing
#206 10426-81 Avenue
Edmonton, Alberta, Canada
T6E 1X5

Canadian Cataloguing in Publication Data

McKeating, Gerald
Birds of Toronto

Includes bibliographical references.
ISBN 0-919433-63-4

1. Birds - Ontario - Toronto 2. Bird watching
- Ontario - Toronto. I. Pluciennik, Ewa, 1954 -
II. Title.
QL685.5.05M234 1990   598.29713'541 C90-091039-9

Cover Design: Ewa Pluciennik
Colour Illustrations: Ewa Pluciennik, Kitty Ho
Black and White Illustrations: Donna McKinnon, Ewa Pluciennik
Book Design and Layout: Yuet Chan, Michael Hawkins, Beata Kurpinski
Editorial: Mary Walters Riskin, Phillip Kennedy
Printing: Kyodo Printing Co. (S'pore) Pte. Ltd., Singapore

Publisher's Acknowledgement
The publisher gratefully acknowledges the assistance of the Federal Department of Communications, Alberta Culture and Multiculturalism, the Canada Council, and the Alberta Foundation for the Literary Arts in the production of this book.

TABLE OF CONTENTS

PREFACE

Most of us have some interest in nature and have been intrigued at one time or another by birds. An unusual duck on the river, a flash of red in the garden, loons at the cottage or the cheerful chickadee at the bird feeder have brought us enjoyment, and perhaps awakened a greater interest in birds. Many people enjoy feeding birds, and like to have them around the garden or cottage. They give us some tangible contact with nature, no matter how slight, in an environment increasingly consumed by urban life.

This book is for people who are not necessarily active birdwatchers, but who just want to know a little bit more about the common birds around them. There are many excellent bird books which are more comprehensive than this: this book is for the casual garden observer and it is hoped that it will provide a stimulus to dig deeper into the fascinating world of birds.

Each bird is illustrated in colour with a brief description of some of the characteristics of the species. An overview of the urban habitats is provided, and some ideas on attracting birds to your property are included. The sequence of species accounts follows the family order presented by W. Earl Godfrey, *Birds of Canada*, revised edition, 1986.

For many years, Ontario has had the benefit of the efforts of many naturalists clubs and dedicated volunteers in the conserving of natural areas and the heightening of awareness of nature. Public interest in the environment has never been greater than it is today, and it is due in part to the efforts of these volunteers. To them, this book is dedicated.

Gerald McKeating

ACKNOWLEDGEMENTS

Many thanks to Dr. Geoffrey Holroyd and Dr. Ian Kirkham for their helpful comments on the manuscript, and to Ewa Pluciennik for her paintings.

Thanks to my wife and fellow birdwatcher, Patricia Crossley, who typed in the manuscript.

I would also like to express my gratitude to the Federation of Ontario Naturalists (FON) for letting us include their helpful *Checklist of Ontario Birds*. The FON is a non-profit wildlife organization with seventy-seven affiliated environmental and natural history groups. The FON's quarterly magazine, *Seasons*, regularly publishes a column on bird behaviour and identification, called "Birder's Notebook." In addition to the *Checklist*, the FON has also published a series of bird recordings, a children's book entitled *Birdwise*, and the *Atlas of Breeding Birds of Ontario*.

Most of all, I would like to recognize the extraordinary contribution of the many naturalists in the Toronto region who have given so much of their time to interest others in the wonderful world of birds.

BIRDS IN THE CITY

FOR ANYONE with an interest in the environment, birds provide a very real and tangible way of identifying with nature. Whether on a busy downtown street or in a remote part of a national park, birds and are easy to see and appreciate — without the need for special knowledge or equipment. Over the last decade more and more people have taken up birdwatching in their spare time and today it is the fastest growing recreational activity in the western world. Whether one actually goes out on a hike to look for birds, or merely appreciates them as part of another recreational activity, birdwatching greatly enhances one's enjoyment of the outdoors.

Many of us live in cities, but this in no way diminishes the possibilities or the pleasures in looking for birds. Birds, like people, have adapted to the urban situation, and their variety and abundance in the city can be a constant source of fascination to anyone who cares to look. Many of the habitats in urban areas resemble natural habitats, while others are strictly urban and attract, in a unique way, their own fauna. Some of the more aggressive and common species, including Rock Doves (Pigeons), Starlings, House Sparrows, and Ring-billed Gulls, have adapted to the human environment, with its structures and its garbage.

The back yard is a good place for birdwatching as here we have the opportunity to bring birds directly into our lives. Even the newest subdivisions will have their bird "pioneers," although the variety of species at first will be small. Older residential neighbourhoods will have many more species because of the greater numbers and types of trees and bushes.

Back yards are by no means the only place in the city to see birds. In some of our parks and open spaces, it is possible to see flycatchers, warblers, and even hawks and owls. Toronto has many river valleys, ravines and shorelines, waiting to be explored.

Downtown city parks can also provide an opportunity to observe birds. Birds such as Rock Doves are of course well known, but I have also enjoyed seeing thrushes, warblers, and sparrows in Queen's Park — right in the heart of downtown. Even Peregrine Falcons have been introduced to the centre of the city.

To appreciate fully the diverse bird life in the Metropolitan region, explore various habitats, each of which has its own bird population. Try the marshes of the Humber River or Pickering, explore the ravines like Cedarvale or Moore Park, visit the Leslie Street Spit or Toronto Islands Park, and especially Hanlan's Point. The Rouge River Valley System in nearby Scarborough is another area rich in bird and other wild life. Do not forget your own neighbourhood. By visiting different habitats, your appreciation and enjoyment of birds will grow with each trip.

HABITATS

The "habitat" of a bird is a place which provides all the basic necessities of life for that bird at some point in its life cycle. The term embraces the diversity of vegetation, nesting cover, food supply, escape routes, water, soils and climate. A habitat has the elements necessary for life. Each bird species has specific needs, and lives in the habitat best suited to its needs.

Wetlands

These wet areas are highly attractive to many species of birds. The habitats are varied, from cattail marshes to wooded swamps. Many of our marshes are bordered by thickets and trees, thereby providing a life zone for the birds as well. Some of our better marshes are associated with the waterfront and river systems of the region. Unfortunately, development has to date eliminated nearly eighty-five percent of southern Ontario's wetland areas.

The marshlands contain ducks, geese, and sometimes Mute

Swans, herons, blackbirds, rails and sparrows. These wetlands can host a multitude of migrants

Rattray Marsh in Port Credit, Humber Valley Park and the marshes associated with the river mouths in Scarborough and Pickering are particularly attractive to birds.

The Waterfront

The Toronto waterfront is great place to find wintering ducks like Oldsquaw and Greater Scaup. Here, in winter, you can see Herring Gulls, Ring-billed Gulls, Great Black-backed Gulls and sometimes Glaucous Gulls. Our permanent population of Canada Geese will be looking for a handout here as well. Grenadier Pond, even though it offers only a small amount of open water, can be filled with ducks.

Various vantage points on Lake Ontario, from Burlington to the downtown harbour, are all excellent for viewing ducks which do not breed in the region but use Lake Ontario as a wintering habitat. Appropriate habitats must be available to birds for each season in the life cycle, and in the case of our wintering ducks, the breeding habitat may be several thousand kilometres away. The Oldsquaw, for example, breeds on the Arctic tundra.

The Leslie Street Spit, or Tommy Thompson Park as it is known, is an example of an artificially-created habitat. Bird habitation of the area, was pioneered by Ring-billed Gulls, which found the ground suitable for nesting. Over time, grasses, trees and shrubs have developed in the area. Now, it is a phenomenal site for birdwatching, with ducks, geese, shorebirds, gulls, terns and songbirds either nesting in the area or using it for a short period of time during migration. The Leslie Street Spit is open to the public year-round on weekends and most holidays.

Ravines and River Valleys

The ravine and valley systems of Metropolitan Toronto provide the region with an extensive network of modified natural areas. A woodland habitat typical of the Great Lakes forest region exists, offering tall white pine, hemlock, American beech, sugar maple, oak and varous shrubs which provide food and shelter for nesting birds and migrants.

The ravines penetrate the urban core like long fingers as they cut through the developed areas. The continuous cover in the ravines provides a safe travel corridor for migrant songbirds in spring. These wild islands also become the nesting homes for birds like Northern Orioles, Least Flycatchers, Red-eyed Vireos, even Great Horned Owls and Pileated Woodpeckers. In winter, they provide refuge for winter finches. Some of my favourite ravines include Moore Park and the Central Don Valley system. These mixed wood areas can contain many of the same species found in more natural wooded areas outside the city. Evergreen belts and conifer woods provide shelter in winter for chickadees, kinglets and owls.

OPEN SPACE

Within our urban area, the open spaces also provide a habitat for birds. Cemeteries like Mount Pleasant are fine places to birdwatch as many of the trees and shrubs have berries and seeds attractive to birds. Hydro transmission rights-of-way provide favourable conditions for field birds like Eastern Meadowlarks and Savannah Sparrows. As well, they can provide a corridor between different kinds of habitats, a linkage that adds to species diversity. Industrial land, gardens, back lanes and the subway right-of-way can provide habitats for some of the more common species. Even larger industrial complexes may provide the necessary elements as the unused area regenerates into natural conditions.

Fallow lands awaiting development provide favourable conditions for many open-country birds. In winter, the fields west of the city are good places to look for birds of prey, as they are attracted to the mice usually found in uncultivated fields.

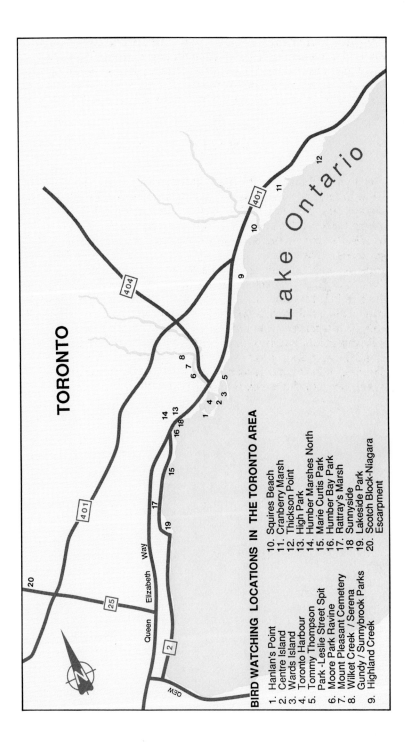

TORONTO

Lake Ontario

QEW

Queen

Elizabeth Way

BIRD WATCHING LOCATIONS IN THE TORONTO AREA

1. Hanlan's Point
2. Centre Island
3. Wards Island
4. Toronto Harbour
5. Tommy Thompson Park - Leslie Street Spit
6. Moore Park Ravine
7. Mount Pleasant Cemetery
8. Wilket Creek / Serena Gundy / Sunnybrook Parks
9. Highland Creek
10. Squires Beach
11. Cranberry Marsh
12. Thickson Point
13. High Park
14. Humber Marshes North
15. Marie Curtis Park
16. Humber Bay Park
17. Rattray's Marsh
18. Sunnyside
19. Lakeside Park
20. Scotch Block-Niagara Escarpment

11

THE DON VALLEY, like many other valleys of the Metropolitan Toronto area, provides diverse habitats for wildlife. Fields, small marshes and woodlands are home to pheasants, cardinals and even Great Horned Owls.

OLDER RESIDENTIAL AREAS with their tall trees and house shrubbery provide havens for orioles, robins, Red-eyed Vireos and Rose-breasted Grosbeaks, among others. The chimneys of the old houses can provide nesting locations for Chimney Swifts.

15

THE ISLANDS and the inner harbour provide a splendid habitat for a number of birds, but Canada Geese are especially important. After nesting, the birds graze on the short grass of the park lawns, the water providing an ideal refuge from disturbance.

16

ABANDONED FARMLAND is an excellent habitat for birds. As the land slowly returns to its wild state, the grasses and flowers, shrubs and trees, can yield goldfinches, Yellow Warblers, Indigo Buntings, Brown Thrashers, and a host of other species. Each species is attracted to a different habitat element within the regenerating field.

19

CEMETERIES are wild oases in the middle of the city, and one of the best places for birdwatching is Mount Pleasant Cemetery. The shrubs and trees attract a multitude of birds from Blue Jays to woodpeckers, and during spring migration, the trees can be alive with warblers.

BIRDS OF TORONTO

KEY TO SYMBOLS

LAKES

URBAN AREAS

RIVER

UNCULTIVATED
FARM LAND

WETLAND

FIELDS, OPENINGS &
CLEARINGS

DECIDUOUS
TREES

RAVINES & VALLEYS

CONIFEROUS
TREES

AMERICAN BITTERN

Botaurus lentiginosus
Butor d'Amérique
larger than crow-sized

THE AMERICAN BITTERN has a most unusual voice, its loud, guttural, three-syllable *pump-er-lunk* being heard from wetlands for a considerable distance. More often heard than seen, its call is reminiscent of the sound of an old-fashioned water pump; it is a sound which is characteristic of marshes in spring.

An expert at fishing, the American Bittern's overall brown colour pattern is excellent camouflage against the marsh vegetation, the bird seemingly frozen with bill outstretched, like an old stake sticking out from the mud.

When feeding, the bird stands motionless along the edge of a shallow pond, eyes concentrating on the water. With amazing speed, the bill is thrust downward to seize the prey, be it a fish, crayfish, frog or snail.

The nest, built by the female, is a platform of dead marsh vegetation placed within the cattails. The four to six eggs are olive-brown to olive-buff and hatch after about twenty-four days of incubation. The young leave the nest when they are about fourteen days old.

GREAT BLUE HERON

Ardea herodias
Grand Héron
larger than gull-sized

WE OFTEN INCORRECTLY CALL our largest heron a crane, but this inhabitant of shallow marshes and ponds around the city is not related to the crane family. A simple way of discriminating between the two birds is to watch them in flight; herons fly with a crook in their neck, while cranes fly with their necks outstretched.

The Great Blue Heron is most often sighted after the breeding season when the adults and immatures are seen standing motionless waiting for a frog, fish or anything else that their spear-like bills can snare.

They nest in colonies of varying sizes. The flattish nest is large and built of sticks, near the tops of trees, and several may be located in one tree.

Although tolerant of human activity, they must have secluded, undisturbed areas to nest, and wetland areas to feed from. The loss of wetlands and woodlots through urbanization may reduce the distribution of the species. As well, humans who have entered breeding colonies have created panic and loss of life among young herons, which will jump from their nests when frightened.

BLACK-CROWNED NIGHT-HERON

Nycticorax nycticorax
Bihoreau à couronne noire
gull-sized

THIS BLACK AND WHITE HERON presents a short, stocky appearance as it patiently waits at the edge of the marsh for an unsuspecting fish or frog. Restricted in distribution, most of the Black-crowned Night-heron's known nesting areas are associated with large bodies of water where it frequents marshes and the edges of lakes and ponds.

Night-herons are well named for they are most active in the evening hours, although it is not uncommon to see them during the day. The species is often seen as a dark silhouette against the sky as it flies from its daytime roost in the trees to its feeding marshes.

The bird nests in small colonies and builds its nest of sticks in trees or sometimes in shrubs. The nesting material is gathered by the male but the nest is built by the female. Usually three to five pale blue-green eggs are laid, with incubation undertaken by both parents.

Night-herons can be observed along the river shores and marshes, especially following the breeding season. Watch for them in the marshes of the Humber River, at Cranberry Marsh or on other marshes located near the lakefront at Pickering. Important nesting colonies are located within Toronto Harbour on the Leslie Street Spit and on Muggs Island.

MUTE SWAN

Cygnus olor
Cygne tuberculé
larger than gull-sized

THIS NATIVE OE EURASIA became a common inhabitant of country estates, city parks and zoos because it was so easily tamed. Over time, some birds escaped and populations became established in the wild. The large size, white colour and graceful lines continue to make it a popular bird to keep in captivity.

As the name suggests, Mute Swans are silent — except when they are irritated or alarmed. Then they hiss and snort and, in an aggressive display, raise their wing feathers to form a hood over the back. They vigorously defend their nesting territories from other water birds and even humans.

Although Mute Swans select mates early, nesting is not attempted until the third year. Most pair bonds are permanent although if a member of the pair dies, re-mating does occur.

They build their immense nests, which can be 1.2 m wide by 1.5 m long or even larger, out of aquatic vegetation. Up to eight or ten greenish-blue eggs may be laid, with incubation lasting 36 to 38 days. Both adults care for the cygnets which remain with their parents until late fall.

Mute Swans flourish in urban areas and they can be readily found in some of the cattail marshes along the Metropolitan Toronto waterfront.

CANADA GOOSE

Branta canadensis
Bernache du Canada
larger than gull-sized

THE SIGHT OF THESE magnificent birds is both thrilling and familiar. Their V-shaped formations and the sound of their honking have come to mean the arrival of spring, or the return of winter.

Believed to mate for life, an adult will seek another mate only upon the death of its partner. Young geese migrate with their parents in the fall and return with them in the spring — the adults presumably acting as guides — and leave them only when they arrive at the nesting grounds. The yearlings do not nest but gather in flocks with other yearlings.

Canada Geese breed in diverse locations, including islands, shorelines, grassy fields and shrubby areas. The nests are built close to water; most are mounds of sticks and grass and other vegetation, with the insides lined with down. Five to six dull white eggs are laid, with incubation by the female. Within twenty-four hours of hatching, the parents lead the goslings to the relative safety of the water.

Large family groups can be seen thoughout the year on the Toronto Islands and almost every other park along the waterfront. While the birds were once quite rare around the turn of the century, they have recovered and are now one of our most abundant species of waterfowl.

AMERICAN BLACK DUCK

Anas rubripes
Canard noir
gull-sized

BLACK DUCKS are fairly common throughout the year along the waterfront. They are much darker than Mallards and lack the Mallards' white outer tail feathers and wing bars. In flight, the white underwings of the Black Duck provide a vivid contrast to the dark body. Mallards and Black Ducks freely hybridize and many of the birds seen around the city will exhibit characteristics of both species. The Mallard genes appear dominant, with subsequent generations looking more like Mallards than Blacks.

The preferred nesting zone of the Black Duck is in the mixed-wood forest of the Canadian Shield, where beaver ponds are a favourite location. In agricultural Ontario, they frequent similar habitats to Mallards.

The diet of the Black is varied due to the multitude of habitats it uses, and includes aquatic vegetation, insects and their larvae, small frogs and tadpoles. A dabbling duck, the bird feeds in shallow water, where it reaches bottom by tipping up the tail and probing the mud with its bill. In southwestern Ontario, waste corn in agricultural fields is an important food source in late fall and throughout the winter.

MALLARD
Anas platyrhynchos
Canard colvert
gull-sized

ANCESTOR TO MOST DOMESTIC DUCKS, the Mallard is the most common and best known duck in the Toronto region. It readily adapts to urban areas from city parks to sewage lagoons while in wilder places it frequents ponds, marshes, lakes and rivers. Look for it along the waterfront, at Grenadier Pond and in the marsh areas throughout the region. Quite tame in city areas, it is wary in the wild.

Dabbling ducks like the Mallard up-end while feeding — unlike diving ducks which, as their name implies, dive for their food. Mallards feed on aquatic vegetation, seeds, grain, insects, and in the city, on the handouts of people. A high protein diet derived from invertebrates is needed in early spring in order for the hens to be in good condition for egg laying.

Mallards nest on the ground near water, and up to fifteen dullish green eggs may be laid, with incubation by the drably-coloured and therefore well-camouflaged female. Young Mallard broods may appear as early as mid-May but should the first nesting attempt fail, a second effort is usually made. Broods can thus be readily observed until mid-summer. After breeding, male Mallards abandon the females, leaving them to care for the young.

BLUE-WINGED TEAL

Anas discors
Sarcelle à ailes bleues
smaller than crow-sized

UNLIKE SOME OTHER DABBLING DUCKS found in the Toronto region, this swift-flying species is highly migratory, wintering as far south as South America. Blue-wings are the first ducks to migrate south in the fall and, in the spring, the last to return.

They make up for their late arrival from the wintering grounds by nesting within a week of their arrival. Grassy areas are preferred for nesting, and nests have been found as far away from water as two kilometres. Nine to twelve buffy white eggs are generally laid. Egg-laying can start when nest building has barely commenced. Ponds with adjacent grassy areas can be favourite sites for nesting on rural estate lots.

This diminutive duck in its handsome breeding plumage gives a splash of colour in spring. The white facial crescent of the male contrasts with its steel-blue head and neck, a unique feature for identification. In flight a blue shoulder patch is visible on the wing; hence its common name.

During the breeding season, Blue-winged Teal are fairly common residents of the marshes and small ponds.

OLDSQUAW

Clangula hyemalis
Canard kakawi
crow-sized

OLDSQUAWS ARE ABUNDANT in our region in winter, frequently gathering in large flocks out on the lake. There is a constant calling amongst these gregarious birds, the males being among the most chattering of ducks. They can often be seen within Toronto harbour or other areas such as Humber Bay.

The majority of Oldsquaws begin to arrive from the Arctic in late October or early November and remain in the Toronto vicinity until May, later than our other wintering duck species. As Oldsquaws nest in greater numbers in the high Arctic than other ducks, their departure is delayed until the ponds begin to melt on the northern tundra.

Oldsquaws are expert divers and are believed to dive deeper in search of food than any other diving duck. Unfortunately, this has resulted in some mortality as they can get caught in fishermen's nets set well below the surface. Animal food such as crustaceans provide the bulk of the Oldsquaw diet.

Oldsquaws have unusual seasonal plumages, mainly white and black in fall and winter, and brown in spring and summer. The males, with their long central tail feathers, and extraordinarily handsome black and white plumage, are unmistakable and brighten our drab Toronto winterscape.

COMMON GOLDENEYE

Bucephala clangula

Garrot à oeil d'or

crow-sized

COMMON GOLDENEYE are characteristic ducks of Ontario's boreal forest. Their northern breeding range is limited only by the availability of trees large enough to have cavities of sufficient size to allow the ducks to nest. The nest cavity can be up to twenty metres from the ground. When the young hatch, they remain in the cavity for only a day or two, then jump up from the nest to the edge of the cavity and flutter down uninjured to the mother below. She gathers her brood and leads them away.

Some people call these ducks "whistlers," a name derived from the whistling sound the birds make while in flight. This is not a vocalization but is caused by the air passing through the birds' wings.

This duck is a common wintering bird in southern Ontario wherever open water exists. The species can easily be seen in Toronto Harbour or other accessible lake areas especially along the western waterfront.

Expert divers, Goldeneyes remain underwater for an average of thirty seconds at a time, and can reach a depth of six metres in search for food.

COMMON MERGANSER

Mergus merganser
Grand Bec-scie
larger than gull-sized

THE COOL, SPARKLING WATERS of the lakes and rivers in the Canadian Shield are favoured by this species during the breeding season. Anyone who spends time in cottage country or regions like Algonquin Park will be familiar with this expert diving duck. The drake, with its blackish green head and black and whitish body, is vividly coloured and the hen, although drab in comparison, has a noticeable crest and a handsome tawny brown head.

The Common Merganser is a fish-eater and its long serrated bill is an excellent aid in catching prey while swimming underwater.

Common Mergansers, which are the largest inland duck found in North America, usually nest in tree cavities but sometimes use ledges or nest on the ground under dense tangles of bushes. Like Goldeneyes, young Mergansers leave the tree cavity by fluttering to the ground. The young can dive soon after hatching. It is not uncommon for broods to mix into groups of twenty or more and be attended by several females.

This species is a common wintering duck in our region, particularly off the park areas west from Sunnyside.

Inset: female

32

RED-TAILED HAWK

Buteo jamaicensis
Buse à queue rousse
crow-sized

THIS SPLENDID BIRD can often be seen in the river valleys. Using the rising air currents, the Red-tailed Hawk soars effortlessly, its reddish-brown tail highlighted against the sky.

Around undeveloped fields, especially in winter, Red-tails can frequently be seen perched on an exposed tree limb or fence post waiting for an unwary mouse or vole to give itself away and become the day's meal. Although they prefer rodents, Red-tails will feed on pigeons in the city, as well as on injured or unsuspecting waterfowl.

Their favoured habitat is open country for hunting, mixed with woodlands in which to nest. This patchwork pattern of landscape is common in many of the agricultural regions of southern Ontario and as a result the bird is common and widely distributed.

A large, bulky stick-nest is usually built in the crotch of a deciduous tree, or occasionally in a white pine. Before the leaves are fully opened, nests may be visible in tree tops. The two to four eggs are incubated mainly by the female, with the male making frequent visits to the nest to feed her. It is believed that pairs mate for life or until the death of one of the pair, when another mate is taken. Like many other raptors, Red-tail females are larger than males.

AMERICAN KESTREL

Falco sparverius
Crécerelle d'Amérique
smaller than robin-sized

THE AMERICAN KESTREL is the smallest and most common North American falcon, and it competes with the Red-tailed Hawk as the most common and widely distributed hawk in Ontario.

The female is larger than the male and has brown wings, whereas the male's wings are blue-grey. They prefer to nest in old woodpecker holes or hollows in trees, but in the city they will use holes in building walls or under roof gables and they take readily to nesting boxes. The male provides all the food for the female during the thirty day incubation of the four to six creamy-brown splotched eggs, and for the family for the thirty-odd days before the young leave the nest.

We can often see this bird hovering over fields while hunting for mice or grasshoppers and crickets. Both along rural roads and in the city, Kestrels can be seen on telephone lines, fence posts and light standards. In the city during winter, Kestrels prey mainly on small birds. The sudden explosion of House Sparrows away from your feeder may well be caused by a Kestrel looking for a meal.

PEREGRINE FALCON
Falco peregrinus
Faucon pèlerin
crow-sized

THIS STREAMLINED, POWERFUL BIRD is not one that you may think of as an urban bird. But thanks to the efforts of wildlife agencies and dedicated individuals working to save it from extinction, reintroductions in the city have been made.

In its natural habitat, the Peregrine builds its nest on cliff faces, frequently in the vicinity of large bird colonies. That food supply is replaced in urban areas by an abundance of pigeons and House Sparrows which are no match for one of the fastest-flying birds in the world.

A Peregrine will nest in the city, often using the ledge of a tall building. Here, its three to five eggs are laid on little more than a scrape in some gravel where they are incubated by both sexes for up to 35 days.

Virtually wiped out by DDT in eastern North America, the Peregrine is making a slow recovery in both cities and wild places of Eastern Canada and the northeastern United States. The continued use of DDT in Central America still poses a threat to its survival.

Peregrines have always been rare, and to see one engage in a spectacular aerial pursuit of prey will not be soon forgotten.

35

RING-NECKED PHEASANT

Phasianus colchicus
Faisan de chasse
larger than gull-sized

THERE IS NO MISTAKING the male pheasant with its gorgeous array of colours and long pointed tail. The bird is native to Asia and the Greek Argonauts were alleged to have brought the original stock to Europe, where it became an important game bird. The first introductions were made in Ontario during the late 1800s.

In rural locations, the bird uses farmland with corn, grain, and weed seeds being important food sources. Grassy areas are used for nesting, with shelterbelts, cattail marshes and farm hedgerows acting as cover. Farming practices which remove such vital cover have eliminated pheasant from much of our region. The ravines and valleys of Toronto still offer sufficient habitat for the bird and are the best areas to look for the species.

Deep snow and ice storms severely limit this bird's ability to survive on its own in the wild, and pheasants will regularly visit ground bird feeders as a result.

Ring-necked Pheasants gather in small flocks during the winter, but they scatter by late winter. The male then struts elegantly before a female, announcing his presence with loud, bantam-like crows and aggressively defending his territory against intruding males. He can have more than one mate, and the first eggs are laid in late April.

SORA

Porzana carolina
Râle de Caroline
robin-sized

YOU WILL HEAR the Sora more often than you will see it: its far-carrying, descending whinny makes the bird's presence known in the marshes of our region. It often calls its own name.

Soras are the most widespread rail in Ontario, but availability of appropriate habitat is the key to the presence of this bird. Continued human disturbance and destruction of the wetlands could threaten the existence of the Sora.

The nest, often situated in dense vegetation at the edge of a wetland, is a small loosely woven basket attached to standing stalks of marsh vegetation a few inches above the water, or constructed on the ground. Eight to thirteen buffy eggs, spotted with brown, are laid.

Rails are expert skulkers and move within the marsh vegetation with great dexterity and daintiness. If disturbed, they frequently prefer to run within the vegetation rather than to fly. Their long toes allow them to walk nimbly across water lily pads.

In summer they eat many aquatic insects, as well as small mollusks. Later in the summer, seeds are often eaten. Strong fliers, Soras have one of the longest migration routes of the rail family, wintering throughout the Caribbean.

AMERICAN COOT
Fulica americana
Foulque d'Amérique
smaller than crow-sized

COOTS CAN BE NOISY birds, their loud *coo-coo-coo-coo* echoing across the marsh both day and night. Grunts, whistles, croaks, and babbling sounds accompanied by much splashing and splattering give ample reason for the phrase, "crazy as a coot."

In our region, the birds seem to prefer large marshes with broader expanses of deeper open water. They are among the first water birds to return in early spring from their wintering grounds in the southern United States.

While feeding, coots can tip up like dabbling ducks in shallow waters yet they are expert divers who seek various aquatic plants or small fishes or tadpoles. Coots bob their heads while swimming, a habit that is a distinctive field mark.

The bird is semi-colonial in its nesting habits with a number of pairs located in the same vicinity. The nest, constructed by both sexes, is usually well concealed. It is built with the stems of marsh plants upon a platform of the same material, and it floats on the water, anchored to emergent plants.

The downy chicks are black with bristle-like orange to red down about the head, neck and shoulders. That colouration together with a bright red, black-tipped bill gives them a clown-like, spectacular appearance.

KILLDEER

Charadrius vociferus
Pluvier kildir
robin-sized

OF ALL THE SHOREBIRDS found in Ontario, the Killdeer is probably the most familiar. It is found in nearly every open area — including pastures, agricultural fields and stream banks. One can find it nesting on golf courses, airports, lawns or on transportation and utility rights-of-way. I have found it utilizing flat, gravel roofs within the city as a nesting site, the roof replicating its nesting habitat of river gravel flats in more natural situations. Its raucous, persistent call brings attention to its name and announces the arrival of spring.

Like most shorebirds, Killdeer nest in a mere shallow depression in the ground, lined with a few pebbles and weeds. The young look exactly like the adults.

Killdeer are famous for their elaborate distraction displays, designed to lead intruders away from the nest or young. The bird moves away from the intruder dragging its tail or wing as if broken and sometimes tumbling as if helpless. If you follow it, the act will continue, always out of reach, until you are a considerable distance from the nest. The distraction display is most prominent just prior to the hatching of the four light buff coloured, black-splotched eggs, or when the young have recently hatched.

SPOTTED SANDPIPER

Actitis macularia
Chevalier branlequeue
smaller than robin-sized

SPOTTED SANDPIPERS and Killdeer probably share the title of the best known and most widely distributed shorebirds in North America. Like other species which are widespread, Spotted Sandpipers are highly adaptable to a variety of habitats. You can find the bird along stream banks, edges of ponds and lake shorelines yet it is readily adaptable to human-altered environments, from agricultural fields to sewage lagoons.

In breeding plumage, the adults have round black dots on their white underside which contrasts with the greyish-brown back. In autumn, these spots are absent.

The nest is a shallow depression in the ground, well hidden, and difficult to find. The male provides most of the incubation and care for the young. Four buffy, spotted brown eggs are laid. As soon as the young hatch, they can run over the ground, bobbing and teetering in a manner similar to their parents. After thirteen to sixteen days, the young can fly.

This common sandpiper appears like a nervous bird with its constant teetering. It bobs its tail almost continuously as it searches for insects along the shore. In flight, the wings are held very stiffly and the wing beats are shallow, giving the appearance of a jerky, nervous flight.

SEMIPALMATED SANDPIPER

Calidris pusilla
Bécasseau semipalmé
larger than sparrow-sized

THESE COMMON SANDPIPERS do not nest within our region but they can be found in large numbers during migration in spring and fall. They are the most abundant sandpiper during this period and possibly the most abundant of all shorebirds within their range. They gather in compact flocks, the bodies seemingly touching, as they probe the mud for worms or aquatic insects. The name is derived from the webbing between their front toes.

This bird is one of the more difficult species of sandpiper to identify. It is similar to several other species that are collectively known as "peep." It is sparrow-sized with the female slightly larger than the male. The legs are black and the bill is short. Experience and comparison with other similar species are the only ways of distinguishing it.

Visit muddy shorelines and marvel at the large flocks whirling through the air, twisting and turning simultaneously in tight formations, not one bird hesitating in the direction of the flight. On the ground when resting, they huddle together, bills tucked into wings, and often standing on one leg.

Sewage ponds, the Leslie Street spit and the marshes of east Metro are good places to see this species.

RING-BILLED GULL

Larus delawarensis
Goéland à bec cerclé
larger than crow-sized

OVER THE PAST NUMBER of years, Ring-billed Gulls have undergone a population explosion to such an extent that they are viewed by many as pests. They take advantage of the many human-created food sources and are adaptable to a variety of habitats. It was estimated in 1984 that 427,000 pairs nested in the Ontario portion of the Great Lakes alone. This large and rapid population increase has created many problems, from damage to agricultural crops to the spoiling of popular recreation areas. Control programs have been instituted at some nesting sites in an attempt to reduce the problem.

Ring-bills, however, also eat large numbers of insects and they are useful scavengers. They are the common interior gull of southern Ontario where they feed in fields on a variety of grubs and worms.

The nest is built on the ground where two to three buffy eggs with various brown spots and blotches are laid. The young swim at an early age, where they take to the water to escape intruders. They will nest on breakwaters, slag heaps and in industrial areas, with the most celebrated colony being established on the Leslie Street Spit, now known officially as Tommy Thompson Park.

HERRING GULL

Larus argentatus
Goéland argenté
gull-sized

THIS IS THE COMMON large "sea gull" of our region, its name alluding to the fish which forms part of its varied diet. The Great Lakes provide a bounteous food resource in the form of alewives, a species of fish that flourishes in our polluted environment. Herring Gulls have also adapted to human garbage as a source of food.

The adult Herring Gull has a blue-grey mantle with black wing-tips. Its legs are flesh-coloured and at close range, you can see a red dot near the tip of its yellow bill. The Ring-billed Gull is similar but smaller, with yellowish legs and a black ring near the tip of the bill. These two gulls are common in our area and can often be seen at very close range in park or waterfront areas.

Herring Gulls utilize a variety of nest sites from undisturbed islands in the Great Lakes, recreational lakes and rivers, to various types of shorelines. Generally, they nest in the same colonies year after year, although they occasionally nest in single pairs. The nest, on the ground, is lined with grass or other vegetation, and two to three eggs of variable colour are laid. Immature Herring Gulls obtain full adult plumage after three years of moults.

43

GREAT BLACK-BACKED GULL

Larus marinus
Goéland à manteau noir
larger than gull-sized

GREAT BLACK-BACKED GULLS are huge, much larger than the more common Herring Gulls found in our area. The snow-white head of the adult contrasts vividly with the black back and wings.

This species is more common in the Gulf of St. Lawrence area than in Ontario. Some birds, however, winter in the Great Lakes region and it is not uncommon to see one perched on the piers and breakwaters along the waterfront.

In recent years, the bird has nested along Lake Ontario in very limited numbers. It is possible that the species may become a better-established breeding bird in the future.

Voracious feeders, Black-backs are aggressive towards other gulls and terns wherever they may share nesting grounds. The eggs and young of other birds are favourite foods.

COMMON TERN

Sterna hirundo
Sterne pierregarin
smaller than crow-sized

COMMON TERNS nest throughout Ontario — usually in colonies — in natural wild areas like the North Channel of Lake Huron, as well as in settings developed by humans, such as the Leslie Street Spit in Toronto. A number of colonies can be found on the St. Lawrence River and Trent-Severn Waterway.

Natural nesting sites can be small, sparsely vegetated islands or gravelly beaches. Terns will also use slag heaps, dredge spoil sites and even structures like piers or breakwaters.

The nest is a shallow depression in the sand and gravel where usually two to three eggs are laid. Although the bird tolerates vegetation, when plants become too dense, the nesting site may be abandoned. As well, Ring-billed Gulls, which are a more aggressive species, begin to nest earlier than terns and can bar the tern from its preferred nesting sites.

While foraging for food, a tern hovers above the water with rapid wing beats. When it spots small fish, it swiftly dives and snatches its prey from the water.

Common Terns can be easily confused with two other tern species, the Arctic Tern and Forster's Tern. These latter two both occur in Ontario, in small numbers; the Arctic Tern, however, is extremely rare in this region.

45

BLACK TERN

Chlidonias niger
Guifette noire
robin-sized

THIS GRACEFUL BIRD is one of the most handsome birds in the gull family. In breeding season, the adults have dark black heads and necks with slate-grey backs, wings and tails.

Black Terns spend much time in the air, hovering buoyantly above the marsh where, swallow-like, they snatch insects from the air. On shallow dives into the water, they pluck small fishes from beneath the surface.

Nests are constructed in cattail marshes or shallow, weedy areas of inland lakes and rivers. The birds nest in loose colonies in semi-open areas within the marsh. The nest is built on a floating mat of dead vegetation, or sometimes on a muskrat house.

Two to three eggs, olive or buff with heavy brown markings are laid, and incubated for twenty-one to twenty-two days. The young are able to leave the nest a few days after hatching but they are vigorously defended by the parents: intruders into a nesting site will be greeted with shrill cries and repeated dive-bombing attacks from the adults.

Black Terns have very specific habitat requirements. Changes in water levels at the nest site and the amount of emergent vegetation are among the factors which determine its desirability. Marsh areas that appear suitable to us are often unoccupied or abruptly abandoned for reasons as yet unknown.

ROCK DOVE

Columba livia
Pigeon biset
smaller than crow-sized

THE UBIQUITOUS ROCK DOVE, or domestic pigeon — found in every city and town and on every farm — needs no introduction. A Eurasian species, it was domesticated by the French and first introduced into North America at Port Royal, Nova Scotia in 1606.

In the natural environment, Rock Doves use caves and cliffs for their nest sites. With the growth of our cities, older houses and modern office and commercial structures have provided many nesting ledges and perches.

The Rock Dove's ready adaptation to human environments, along with its ability to nest in any month and to raise two or three families a year, has allowed the species to become firmly established throughout many parts of the world.

Two white eggs are laid in a flimsily constructed nest of sticks or twigs. After seventeen to nineteen days the young hatch and are fed "pigeon milk," a substance produced in the crop of the parents. When older, weed seeds, garbage and some berries are eaten.

One of the swiftest birds in flight, Rock Doves are relatively tame in the city but retain a wildness in rural situations, taking flight on the least disturbance.

MOURNING DOVE

Zenaida macroura
Tourterelle triste
smaller than crow-sized

THE DISTINCTIVE COOING of this bird, which can be heard from some distance, is more mellow than sad. Mourning Doves are common in our rural areas, especially in shelterbelts, woodlots and agricultural fields. City neighbourhoods may also contain a pair where adequate cover exists.

The bird is highly adaptive and can easily be found. It has a habit of perching in the open on wires, TV antennas and poles, or on the ground along roadsides, where it seeks gravel to aid in its digestion. It eats enormous amounts of weed and grass seed and, in rural areas, the waste grain left after harvest.

Mourning Doves prefer to nest in coniferous trees but will readily use deciduous trees as well. The nest is flimsy, made of small twigs in the form of a loose platform. It may be constructed on top of an old nest of some other species.

Two pure white eggs are usually laid. After an incubation of fifteen days, the young hatch and are at first fed "pigeon milk." Afterwards, the parents regurgitate seeds to feed the young. In our area, two broods are common in a mating season.

Given adequate food and shelter, Mourning Doves can remain in the region throughout the winter months.

GREAT HORNED OWL

Bubo virginianus
Grand-duc d'Amérique
smaller than gull-sized

SAVAGE AND POWERFUL, the Great Horned Owl has no natural predators, although illegal shooting and trapping present a formidable threat. The owl is an opportunistic feeder: rabbits, mice, rats, squirrels, skunks, grouse and ducks are among its varied menu, and it will even tackle a porcupine. The undigestible portions of its prey are regurgitated in the form of pellets.

Found throughout Canada to the northern tree line, the Great Horned Owl is the most familiar owl in Ontario. Its habitat consists of woodlots of both coniferous and deciduous trees, and its soft hooting can be heard within the ravines of the city as early as January.

Active nests of Great Horned Owls may be discovered in February or early March. Incubation takes thirty days. Young birds can remain in the nest for about fifty days, after which the nearly flightless young spend a few weeks on the ground or low branches in the nesting territory. Young owls found during this period have not been abandoned, and should be left alone.

Crows — which hate owls — will gather in large flocks and caw as loudly as possible to harrass a roosting owl. Watch for this phenomenon. Often when you see a large, noisy group of crows, an owl will be nearby.

49

SNOWY OWL

Nyctea scandiaca
Harfang des neiges
larger than gull-sized

ONE OF THE MOST DISTINCTIVE owls, this resident of the world's Arctic tundras may be found in our region only during the winter months. Some years, major flights into southern Ontario occur, events which indicate a shortage of the Snowy Owl's main food source in the far north, the lemming.

When wintering here, Snowy Owls frequent areas that are outwardly similar to the barren country of the tundra: open agricultural land, and especially fields where rodents abound. They often perch on fence posts, hay bales or other elevated areas during the day, watching for mice and other small mammals.

The Pearson International Airport, Leslie Street Spit, and the shoreline are other likely locations to look for them. However, when major flights occur, Snowy Owls may be seen in industrial areas or even on TV aerials or utility poles in suburban areas.

The Snowy Owl possesses a luxurious feather coat which protects it from the extreme cold. Feathers cover its feet to the tips of the toes. The owl is so well feathered that only its yellow eyes are fully exposed.

This powerful bird is one of the largest and heaviest of our owls, the female being larger than the male.

50

NORTHERN SAW-WHET OWL

Aegolius acadicus
Petite Nyctale
larger than sparrow-sized

THE SAW-WHET OWL is the smallest owl found in eastern Canada. Active from dusk through the nighttime hours, Saw-whets are motionless and appear tame during the day. Finding one, however, is difficult, as they roost in dense tangles of tree cover, or in tree cavities.

In the Toronto region, the bird is most likely to be found during migration in October, as it moves along the Lake Ontario shore. The dense bush found in the nature reserve behind the water filtration plant on Toronto Island is a favourite location.

Breeding takes place in the mixed coniferous and deciduous woodlands of the Canadian Shield. Here, the bird nests in old woodpecker holes or natural tree cavities, with egg laying commencing in early April. The five or six white eggs are incubated primarily by the female.

Early in the breeding season, Saw-whets call frequently. They possess a variety of calls, one of which resembles the filing of a saw: hence the name. Its most common call is a monotonous series of clear, metallic, one-syllabled notes, repeated incessantly. After nesting has begun, the birds become quiet.

The diet consists of mice and smaller mammals like chipmunks or red squirrels. Insects are taken too, as well as the occasional small bird.

COMMON NIGHTHAWK

Chordeiles minor
Engoulevent d'Amérique
smaller than robin-sized

OFTEN HEARD on warm summer evenings over the cities and towns of southern Ontario, the Common Nighthawk is one of our more familiar summer birds.

Common Nighthawks are easy to identify from their behavioural characteristics: voracious insect eaters, they feed at dusk or at night on the hordes of insects attracted by the lights of our cities and towns. Even on Yonge Street, the birds frequent the night sky just above streetlamp level, oblivious to the noise and confusion below.

The flight is graceful but highly erratic as insects are swept out of the air. Often the bird utters a distinctive nasal *peent*, a familiar call to many of us. Nighthawks engage in spectacular aerial displays during courtship and at the end of a steep nose-dive a muffled boom sometimes occurs, created by the air rushing through the wings.

In cities and towns, flat gravelled building roofs provide ideal nesting habitat. In more natural environments, nighthawks nest in open, gravelly soil areas of pastures, burned-over tracts of forest, clearings or beaches, and on dry river beds.

Two variably coloured eggs are laid directly upon the ground. After about nineteen days of incubation the young hatch and are fed by the parents' regurgitation of previously caught food.

CHIMNEY SWIFT

Chaetura pelagica
Martinet ramoneur
smaller than sparrow-sized

THE CHIMNEY SWIFT is virtually always in flight in daylight, and is common above our city skyline. Its silhouette resembles a "flying cigar," with wings engaged in a constant jerky motion: it does not intentionally land on the ground.

Swifts are well named, for their flight is indeed rapid: they zig-zag across the sky at heights which range from just above our homes, to levels that make them appear to be mere specks. While in flight they constantly utter a "skittering" call, which can be readily heard on the ground. All food is caught on the wing, and they drink by touching the water surface lightly with the bill. Even nesting material is snapped off by hovering close to a twig.

The birds do utilize chimneys for nesting and as places to roost. Those of large homes in our older residential neighbourhoods are ideal for this purpose. While roosting, swifts cling with their sharp nails to the chimney walls. In large groups they may overlap each other like rows of shingles.

The nest is cemented together and attached to the wall by the glutenous saliva of the bird. The young first fly thirty days after hatching and return to the nest after the first flight.

Surprisingly, in evolutionary terms swifts are closely related to hummingbirds, both species having very small feet and long, narrow wings.

RUBY-THROATED HUMMINGBIRD

Archilochus colubris
Colibri à gorge rubis
smaller than sparrow-sized

THE RUBY-THROATED HUMMINGBIRD is the smallest bird found in Ontario, its body probably no longer than the end joint of your thumb.

Because of their small size, hummingbirds have the highest metabolism or "food burning" of any warm-blooded vertebrate animal in the world, and must feed continuously in daytime to stay alive. They feed on minute insects and nectar obtained from brightly coloured flowers. In addition, they are attracted by the sap which oozes from the drill-holes of Yellow-bellied Sapsuckers, and to the insects that become stuck in the sap.

The Ruby-throat feeds at many flowers: both wild species, like fireweed and jewelweed, and common garden plants such as columbine, honeysuckle and salvia. As well, they take readily to hummingbird feeders. They possess an extensile tongue which can reach deep into the flower, drill-hole or feeder.

The nest is built on the limb or twig of a tree. It is a construction marvel composed of bud scales, plant down and silk or webbing from tent caterpillars and spiders, decorated outside with small bits of lichen. Two, white, bean-sized eggs are laid, with all incubation and raising of young being left to the female.

The adult male has a bright iridescent throat that can appear blackish but which flashes deep red or orange when caught by the sun.

BELTED KINGFISHER
Ceryle alcyon
Martin-pêcheur d'Amérique
larger than robin-sized

OF 86 SPECIES of kingfisher in the world, this is the only one found in Canada. It has a striking appearance, and the female is more colourful than the male, a characterisic unusual in North American birds. Both sexes are blue-grey above but in addition to the broad band of blue-grey across the breast, the female also has a chestnut band and rufous flanks. A conspicuous bird, we often hear its harsh rattling call before we see it.

Kingfishers can perch motionless on a dead limb above the water for long periods, watching for prey. When a small fish is sighted, the bird dives below the water's surface, seizing the fish in its strong bill.

Kingfishers excavate long horizontal burrows into eroded river or lake banks for nesting. Sometimes the bird will select gravel pits or road and railway cut-backs, as long as the location is close to water. It may take the bird up to three weeks to create the burrow, digging the hole with its bill then pushing the soil out with its feet. Usually six or seven white eggs are laid, and in-cubated primarily by the female.

In our region, Kingfishers can be found in many of the river valleys or quiet pond areas. Even in winter, an occasional Kingfisher remains, as long as open water is present.

YELLOW-BELLIED SAPSUCKER

Sphyrapicus varius
Pic maculé
smaller than robin-sized

THE YELLOW-BELLIED SAPSUCKER is well named. Its small drill-holes (about 0.5 cm in diameter) in vertical or horizontal rows in trees are ummistakable. When the sap begins to fill the shallow holes, the sapsucker uses its long, extensile, brush-tipped tongue to lick up the sap and the insects which are attracted to it. This food supply also attracts hummingbirds and warblers. A variety of insects, including forest tent caterpillars, are also eaten by sapsuckers.

The long white stripe which extends down each folded wing is diagnostic. There are no other sapsucker species in Ontario.

The bird prefers second growth forest: white birch is preferred as a food source and poplar, because of its soft inner core, is ideal for nest excavation. Usually the tree is still alive but the heartwood has begun to decay.

The male does most of the nest excavation in which five or six white eggs are laid. Incubation is done by both parents, with the male usually on the nest at night.

During migration, the bird is common in wooded areas of our region; however, it is a more common breeding bird around estate lots or in the cottage country of southern Ontario where its preferred trees are more common.

DOWNY WOODPECKER
Picoides pubescens
Pic mineur
sparrow-sized

DOWNY WOODPECKERS are common permanent residents throughout most of Ontario, north to the southern edge of the Hudson Bay lowlands. Found throughout the wooded areas of the city, they are welcome and frequent winter visitors to backyard feeding stations. Watch for them in ravines, woodlots and in older neighbourhoods where deciduous trees grow. They are sometimes also found in open fields, searching on mullein stalks or drilling on goldenrod galls for insect larvae.

Our smallest woodpecker, the Downy is almost identical in plumage to the larger Hairy Woodpecker, which has a longer, heavier bill. The males of both species have a small red patch on the back of the head that is lacking in the females.

The long drumming of male woodpeckers, so often heard in spring, is a territorial announcement and also serves to attract females for courtship.

Although the Downy Woodpecker is a well-known bird in urban gardens in winter, it is much more reclusive during the breeding season. Both sexes share in digging the gourd-shaped nesting cavity, which may be as deep as twenty to thirty centimetres, in a dead tree or snag. Four to five white eggs are usually laid and incubation is about twelve days.

NORTHERN FLICKER

Colaptes auratus
Pic flamboyant
larger than robin-sized

ONE OF OUR BEST KNOWN woodpeckers, the Northern Flicker is conspicuous by its large white rump patch and yellowish underwing. Its audible call, undulating flight and habit of probing the ground for ants, aid in identification. Sexes are similar but the adult female lacks the black moustache patch.

Flickers select a variety of habitats but prefer open, wooded areas. They may readily be seen in our parks, ravines or in older residential neighbourhoods containing larger trees. Some hardy individuals overwinter in our region.

Northern Flickers nest in tree cavities, and either excavate a new hole or use an existing one from a previous year. They will also use cavities in fence posts or telephone poles, and sometimes nest in "flicker nest boxes" put up in backyards or gardens especially for them. Competition from starlings for the nest box may, however, be a disadvantage. In more northern areas, old flicker holes may be used by other cavity-nesting species such as Bufflehead ducks. Due to their preference for open areas, Northern Flicker nest sites can often be viewed from a distance with little interference to the bird.

Six to eight glossy white eggs are laid atop the fresh woodchips in the cavity. After incubation by both sexes for about eleven to twelve days, the young hatch.

PILEATED WOODPECKER

Dryocopus pileatus
Grand Pic
larger than crow-sized

A LOUD, POWERFUL CALL announces the presence of the spectacular Pileated Woodpecker, and its powerful, echoing drumming on a dead tree or stub advertises its territory. For such a large, noisy bird, it can be elusive: we often get only a glimpse of it as it flies across a road or through the woods.

Formerly scarce, the species has made a comeback as second growth forests have matured. Although it prefers more extensive tracts of forest, the bird readily adapts to city parks, ravines and other areas containing mature trees. Once established, the bird defends its territory against other Pileated Woodpeckers throughout the year. During the winter months, it may visit the suet at your bird feeder.

Three to four white eggs are laid in a cavity excavated in a dead tree, between four and twenty-one metres from the ground. The nest site may be revealed by a pile of woodchips at the base of the tree. As with other species of woodpecker, the young are highly vocal and will give the location of the nest away.

Pileated Woodpeckers chisel large vertical cavities in tree trunks and utility poles in pursuit of food and are sometimes accused of causing severe damage. In fact, the trees and poles are often infested with carpenter ants, a favourite food of the bird.

EASTERN WOOD PEWEE

Contopus virens
Pioui de l'Est
larger than sparrow-sized

THE EASTERN WOOD PEWEE is a common flycatcher of our open woodlands in rural areas, urban parks and the ravine and valley systems. It can be distinguished from other dull-coloured flycatchers by its larger size, darker colouration and less greenishness. It lacks the obvious eye-ring of other flycatchers but it has distinct wing bars.

An inhabitant of the canopy of tall trees, the bird is more often heard than seen. It has a distinctive song; its plaintive *pee-wee*, dropping in pitch, announces its presence. Even on the hottest, most humid days, pewees continue to call, long past the period when most birds have stopped singing for the season.

The Eastern Wood Pewee forages like other flycatchers, eating a wide variety of insect life. Some berries are also eaten in late summer.

The nest, which is high in the treetops, is hard to find. Made of grasses and other similar fibres, it is fastened onto a horizontal branch, and its outside is covered with lichens. Usually three creamy white eggs, with brown markings towards the larger end, are laid. The eggs hatch after about thirteen days incubation.

The species seems ubiquitous, and is found anywhere, in parks or by the summer cottage.

LEAST FLYCATCHER

Empidonax minimus
Moucherolle tchébec
sparrow-sized

ALTHOUGH IT IS OUR SMALLEST FLYCATCHER, the Least is quite similar to several other species, even to the experienced eye. In the field it is best identified by its frequent *chebec* call, which is often repeated. Fortunately, the other flycatchers also have distinctive calls, and this is the best way to distinguish the species.

Least Flycatchers are fairly common summer residents in second growth woodlands throughout the city and surrounding countryside. They like the woodland edge or forest openings and can be seen in woodlots, ravines and city parks. In mature, treed neighbourhoods, the fragmentation of the vegetation provides the bird with a good habitat.

The nest is usually built in the crotch of a branch in a small hardwood tree. Tall shrubs like alder, red osier dogwood and willow are also used. Four creamy white eggs are laid, in the thin-walled cup nest. The female incubates the eggs for about fourteen days, during which time she is sometimes fed by the male.

Like other flycatchers, the Least will perch on an exposed twig or post and dart out to catch passing insects. It also catches insects by scrambling about the bark and leaves of trees.

This bird is more likely to inhabit our gardens than other species of flycatcher.

EASTERN PHOEBE

Sayornis phoebe
Moucherolle phébi
sparrow-sized

MOST OF OUR SMALL FLYCATCHERS are dull-coloured and the Eastern Phoebe is no exception. Its most noticeable habit is that of "wagging" its tail when it alights upon a perch — the tail is swept down and up, a field characteristic of importance in identification. In addition, it calls its name quite distinctly with the accent on the first syllable: *fee-be*, repeated over and over.

Depending on the weather, Eastern Phoebes can appear as early as late March or early April, making them a welcome harbinger of spring.

The Eastern Phoebe is one of our hardiest flycatchers found near or adjacent to water. While it passes through the city on migration, it is more common as a breeder in the rural areas and throughout cottage country. Old farmhouses, the eaves of cottages, and most characteristically, the beams of country road bridges or footbridges crossing small streams are favoured nesting locations.

The five white eggs are laid in a bulky nest constructed of mud, leaves, grasses and other material. Sometimes the bird will construct a second nest on top of the old one in a subsequent year, or it may repair and re-use the former nest.

In locations where there are few buildings or bridges, the species is uncommon but will nest on the faces of rocky cliffs.

GREAT CRESTED FLYCATCHER

Myiarchus crinitus
Tyran huppé
smaller than robin-sized

THE GREAT CRESTED FLYCATCHER, common throughout southern Ontario, is a very handsome bird. It often frequents the upper branches of mature trees and spends much time foraging for insects in the tree canopy. Its loud call is often heard but the bird is sometimes hard to spot, obscured by the leaves of the tall trees. Like other flycatchers, it darts swiftly out from its perch to snatch dragonflies, moths and other flying insects.

The species is a cavity-nester in deciduous trees. It prefers natural tree cavities but also uses abandoned woodpecker holes. As well, Great Crested Flycatchers will nest in bird boxes. Within the cavity or bird box, a cup-like nest is built of leaves, moss, grass, pine needles and other miscellaneous litter. Curiously, it often uses cast-off snake skins.

Most often, four to six creamy eggs with various handsome brownish patterns are laid. Incubation of the eggs is done by the female with the young hatching after thirteen to fifteen days.

Look for this bird in the ravines and woodlots both in and outside of the city. Parks with mature trees are also likely locations. Like many insect-eating birds, the Great Crested Flycatcher spends only a short period of time in Ontario, arriving in May and departing by early September.

EASTERN KINGBIRD

Tyrannus tyrannus
Tyran tritri
smaller than robin-sized

THE EASTERN KINGBIRD IS PUGNACIOUS, fearlessly attacking crows, hawks, and other larger birds that may pass through its territory. The intruders are often vigorously pursued for some distance, until the kingbird is satisfied that there is no further threat.

The Eastern Kingbird has a crown patch of red on its black head, which is not often seen in normal viewing. A large flycatcher, it is conspicuous through its habit of perching in open places on fences, posts or exposed tree limbs. From there, it darts out to pick off flying insects, often with an audible snap of the bill. When in flight, its short quick wing beats give it a quivering appearance. Quite a vocal bird, it utters many high-pitched notes.

In our region, the Eastern Kingbird is seen along farm hedge-rows, roadsides, old pasture fields or other open areas with scattered trees. Its nest is built well out on a horizontal tree limb, sometimes in shrubs or stumps, more often in flooded areas where dead snags abound. The nest may be poorly concealed, as the bird probably relies on its aggressiveness to ward off intruders.

Three to five whitish eggs, irregularly spotted or blotched with brown, are laid. Following twelve to thirteen days of incubation, the young hatch and after a similar time period the young leave the nest.

HORNED LARK

Eremophila alpestris
Alouette cornue
larger than sparrow-sized

ON OUR OPEN FARM FIELDS and roadside verges the Horned Lark thrives. The majority of its diet consists of weed seeds, and it can be very conspicuous in winter as large groups descend upon one weed patch and boil over to another.

A rugged bird, the Horned Lark winters in southwestern Ontario and adjacent northern United States, and when the flocks begin to move northward in early February, its high tinkling song is a welcome harbinger of spring.

The only member of the lark family that is native to North America, it is found throughout Canada from the prairies to the Arctic tundra. In our region, fallow farm land and extensive open areas such as airfields are reliable places to see the bird.

The "horns" of the Horned Lark are small black feathers on the head which are difficult to see. The bird runs or walks, rather than hopping like other birds, and has an obvious undulating flight.

The nest is built of grasses and similar vegetation in dry open spaces in a depression in the ground. Three to five greyish eggs, with thick brown spots, are laid. The young leave the nest before they are able to fly but they are cared for by the parents for several more days.

PURPLE MARTIN

Progne subis
Hirondelle noire
larger than sparrow-sized

THE PURPLE MARTIN is our largest swallow. A noisy, colonial-nesting bird, it is familiar in town, city and especially in cottage country where it returns year after year to the same nest. The provision of "apartment house" nest boxes has enabled the Purple Martin to be more widely distributed, and instances of its nesting in natural conditions in Ontario are almost unknown.

The female selects the room in an apartment house colony, and the male defends it from other birds. Both sexes construct a nest of grasses, bark, leaves and other material. Four to five dull white eggs are laid, with incubation by the female. After the young can fly, the martins abandon the nest box and range more widely.

Martin houses should be erected in suitable open areas five to six metres up, atop a pole. As House Sparrows and Starlings compete with Purple Martins for the nest box, the martin house should be taken down in fall and re-erected in late April, when the martins return from the south.

The Purple Martin feeds over water, marshes and open spaces, catching a wide variety of flying insects. However, its legendary power at controlling mosquitoes is overrated.

Several of the major parks around the city have martin houses, including High Park and West Humber Park.

TREE SWALLOW
Tachycineta bicolor
Hirondelle bicolore
sparrow-sized

THE EARLIEST SWALLOW to return in spring, a few Tree Swallows are often back in Toronto by late March, with the majority returning in early April.

The bright, iridescent steely-blue back and white underparts distinguish this from all other adult swallow species in Ontario. Its graceful flight over ponds, marshes and fields is a familiar sight, as the bird forages for insects.

Tree Swallows nest in tree cavities or old woodpecker holes, and make extensive use of bird boxes erected in open habitat such as on fences along fields. Flooded wooded areas like those created by beaver dams or areas with lots of standing dead timber offer choice nesting sites.

The bird will tolerate close neighbours and it is not unusual for nest boxes to be occupied by Tree Swallows even when they are placed in relatively close proximity to one another. A nest of grass lined with feathers is constructed inside the box or cavity. Four to six white eggs are laid, with incubation being undertaken by both sexes for between thirteen and sixteen days.

You can often see the male Tree Swallow perching for long periods on a fence or wire near the nest box. The bird readily enters the box when intruders are nearby, but may greet unwelcome visitors with vigorous chattering and aggressive defensive diving.

BARN SWALLOW

Hirundo rustica
Hirondelle des granges
sparrow-sized

ONE OF THE MOST widely distributed bird species, the Barn Swallow nests not only throughout most of North America, but also in Europe and Asia, where the species is known simply as the Swallow.

Named for their preference for barns, old houses, outbuildings and other human structures as nest sites, Barn Swallows are familiar around the cottage where their constant chattering and boathouse droppings can be a source of irritation during breeding season. Nests are even occasionally found on mobile structures, including larger boats such as highway ferries.

Barn Swallows nest as single pairs or in loose colonies. The birds gather mud in their bills, mixed with some vegetation, and plaster it upon a beam or wall. They may take one to two weeks to construct the cup-shaped nest. Four to six white eggs, spotted with reddish brown, are laid, with the female doing most of the incubation.

In August, swallows begin to gather in large numbers, covering the wires and fence lines, but by September most have departed for their wintering grounds in South America.

BLUE JAY
Cyanocitta cristata
Geai bleu
robin-sized

THE SENTINEL OF OUR WOODS and neighbourhoods, this bold, raucous and strikingly handsome bird announces its presence with its screaming call. Its voice is extremely varied, from the loud familiar jay call to soft, barely audible notes.

Although noisy for most of the year, it falls silent during the nesting season, a characteristic quite different from other songbirds. The nest can be built in a variety of situations but evergreens seem to be preferred. The nest itself is quite bulky, being made of sticks, moss and a variety of other items. Four to six greenish or bluish eggs dotted with spots of brown are laid, and incubated by the female for seventeen or eighteen days.

An inhabitant of mixed or deciduous woods, jays can be found practically everywhere. They have adapted well to the urban environment, and gardens with ornamental shrubs and trees, particularly oak and beech, are much to their liking.

Blue Jays will eat almost anything, including acorns, beech nuts, berries, insects and birds' eggs. At feeders, they are particularly fond of peanuts and sunflower seeds.

Some Blue Jays are permanent residents but spectacular migration flights do occur. In September, huge flocks move southwest along the Lake Erie shore where sometimes thousands can be seen. The old Lake Ontario shoreline below St. Clair Avenue is an occasional route.

AMERICAN CROW
Corvus brachyrhynchos
Corneille d'Amérique
crow-sized

ADAPTABLE AND RESOURCEFUL, crows can often be found taking advantage of human rubbish: foraging through garbage cans and landfill sites, and scouring lanes and streets. They eat large numbers of insects and just about anything else they can find, and are frequent predators of birds' eggs.

The American Crow prefers open areas for foraging and wooded areas for roosting and nesting. The largest populations can be found in the agricultural areas that surround the city, the mix of woodlot and open space being ideal to their needs. The crow has benefitted immensely from human land use practices.

The nest is a bulky assemblage of sticks lined with soft grass. Old nests are often refurbished and can become quite large. Usually four to six greenish-blue eggs, splotched with brown, are laid, and incubated by both sexes.

The American Crow is not protected by law and has been persecuted throughout the country. Despite this, it has maintained or increased its numbers; a consequence of its resourcefulness.

Crows gather in large flocks prior to migration. In our region, many do not move far and can be found throughout the winter in huge numbers in Essex and Kent counties.

BLACK-CAPPED CHICKADEE

Parus atricapillus
Mésange à tête noire
smaller than sparrow-sized

ONE OF THE MOST COMMON birds of the city, the Black-capped Chickadee is possibly the most popular as well. Easily attracted to the bird feeder, some individuals act tame and will flutter to your hand for a nut or sunflower seed.

Even on the coldest days of winter, a ravine or wooded area can be filled with the good-natured calls of a winter flock. Chickadees seem to be constantly on the move as they search the branches and bark for insect eggs; however, they do maintain specific winter territories. The flocks disband in early spring with one or two dominant males setting up breeding territories in the former winter flock area.

The whistled *fee-bee* song that begins in mid-winter gives us optimism that spring is not far behind. The bird's more common *chicka-dee-dee-dee* is heard throughout the year.

Chickadees nest in tree cavities, usually not far from the ground, often excavated in rotten stumps or branches. Soft materials line the cavity to form the nest in which six to eight dull white and spotted eggs are laid. Chickadees are quiet and secretive around the nest site, from the start of egg-laying until the young leave the nest.

Chickadees forage in a variety of habitats and like garden landscapes with a mix of shrubbery, evergreens and deciduous trees.

71

RED-BREASTED NUTHATCH

Sitta canadensis
Sittelle à poitrine rousse
smaller than sparrow-sized

WHITE-BREASTED NUTHATCH

Sitta carolinensis
Sittelle à poitrine blanche
smaller than sparrow-sized

NUTHATCHES HAVE A VERY DISTINCTIVE SHAPE and this together with their habit of feeding head down as they move from the top of a tree trunk to the bottom makes them easy to identify. This odd feeding angle may have evolved to allow them to exploit the bark of trees for insect larvae that other birds have missed.

Both species can be found in the city but the White-breasted is more common. Large numbers of Red-breasted Nuthatches can be seen, however, in migration. The latter species is found in association with coniferous trees while the larger White-breasted Nuthatch is more common on deciduous trees. Both species will readily visit feeding stations.

Nuthatches nest in holes in trees which they sometimes excavate themselves. They often use natural cavities and old woodpecker holes. The Red-breasted Nuthatch has the unusual habit of smearing pitch from coniferous trees around the nest-hole entrance with its bill.

Red-breasted Nuthatch populations have likely increased in recent times due to the proliferation of conifer plantations.

Top: Red-breasted Nuthatch
Bottom: White-breasted Nuthatch

73

BROWN CREEPER
Certhia americana
Grimpereau brun
smaller than sparrow-sized

THIS BROWN-AND-WHITE streaked bird is well named: it creeps up tree trunks searching bark crevices for insects with its long curved bill, while bracing itself with its tail against the trunk. When it reaches the top of one tree, it flies down to the bottom of the next and repeats the process. This brief flight is often the only clue to its presence, for its colouration is excellent camouflage against the bark.

Brown Creepers prefer mature woodlands, both hardwoods and conifers. Flooded areas are especially favoured for the hanging bark of dead trees offers ideal sites for its crescent-shaped nest. On rare occasions the nest may be constructed in a tree cavity.

Uncommon in summer, the bird at times seems abundant during its migration in April, when wooded parks, river valley systems and well-treed neighbourhoods can seem almost overrun by Brown Creepers. Some birds can be found with flocks of chickadees in winter.

HOUSE WREN

Troglodytes aedon
Troglodyte familier
smaller than sparrow-sized

NOT AS COMMON as some other city birds, House Wrens have nevertheless adapted well to the urban environment. A backyard with thick shubbery can often contain a pair of House Wrens, and they will be attracted to a nest box set among the bushes in a quiet corner.

House Wrens sing with great energy throughout the day, a pleasant, rapid, chattering song which is easily recognized. They often scold, usually at nothing in particular.

This is the most common, and plainest, wren in eastern North America. Its small size, brown upperparts and stubby tail identify it as a wren. During migration, Winter Wrens pass through the region, but they usually spend the breeding season north of the agricultural area of southern Ontario. Winter Wrens are smaller and they have a definitive eyebrow stripe.

House Wrens utilize cavities as nest sites as well as readily accepting nest boxes. Two broods are raised in a season, and sometimes three. During the nesting period, wrens often change mates between broods. Male House Wrens sometimes maintain more than one mate at a time, overlapping the breeding so that they can help feed both broods, one after the other.

MARSH WREN

Cistothorus palustris
Troglodyte des marais
smaller than sparrow-sized

CATTAIL MARSHES along the lakeshore are home to this noisy bird. It prefers larger marshes interspersed with areas of open water, such as those found in eastern Scarborough and Pickering. Any wren found in a cattail marsh in our region likely belongs to this species. A similar species, the Sedge Wren, does not frequent cattail habitats.

Although the bird tends to be elusive, you can still find it without difficulty. It sings almost constantly, its loud, bubbly, staccato-like song giving away its presence, sometimes even at night.

Marsh Wrens can occupy the same breeding area year after year. They are gregarious birds, often nesting in loose colonies. The nest is a hollow ball of vegetation lashed onto the stems of cattails. An opening is left in the side of the nest as an entrance, and the interior is lined with softer material. The female constructs the real nest but the male builds several dummy nests nearby, the purpose of which is unclear. Five to six dull brown, spotted eggs are laid.

Like other species in southern Ontario which rely on wetlands, Marsh Wrens, though locally common, are absent from much of agricultural Ontario. As wetlands are drained, filled and converted to other uses, Marsh Wren populations will decline.

GOLDEN-CROWNED KINGLET

Regulus satrapa
Roitelet à couronne dorée
smaller than sparrow-sized

KINGLETS ARE TINY, active, inconspicuous birds. The Golden-crown is a small plump bird, olive-green and grey, and the centre of its crown — orange rimmed by yellow in the male, yellow in the female — is bordered by black. These birds never seem to be still, frequently flicking their wings as they forage through the tree branches. At times they seem oblivious to human presence.

A more common breeding bird in northern Ontario than in southern areas, the Golden-crowned Kinglet can be abundant during migration. Small numbers remain in winter, and can be found with flocks of chickadees.

Golden-crowned Kinglets are most common in mature conifer stands, especially where spruce is the predominant tree. They inhabit the upper portions of dense conifers where they build a nest of mosses, lichens and bark. Usually eight or nine very tiny eggs are laid.

The Kinglet's call is a very highly pitched *tsee-tsee-tsee*. Outside the range of some people's hearing capabilities, it can be easily missed.

WOOD THRUSH
Hylocichla mustelina
Grive des bois
robin-sized

THIS RETIRING THRUSH is a summer resident of the mature deciduous trees in our ravines. It is best known for its clear, melodic, bell-like song, heard mainly in the early morning and in the evening. The Wood Thrush is often one of the earliest songsters, frequently sounding its first notes before dawn.

It can be distinguished from other thrushes by its tawny or russet head, which contrasts with its brown back and tail. Its white underparts are heavily spotted with large, black oval dots.

Most of its time is spent on or near the ground. Beetles, caterpillars and grasshoppers are among the variety of insect species it finds amid the woodland litter and the foliage of trees.

The nest is constructed in the crotch of a tree, sapling or shrub, or fixed upon a branch, frequently at a convenient height for viewing. The female incubates the three or four greenish-blue eggs, the colour of which is not unlike the eggs of robins. Both parents feed the young, which leave the nest when they are twelve or thirteen days old.

One of the most restful, sweetish sounds in nature is the song of the Wood Thrush and recalling it during a bleak Toronto winter will bring fond memories of early summer morning strolls.

AMERICAN ROBIN
Turdus migratorius
Merle d'Amérique
robin-sized

FAMILIAR TO ALMOST EVERYONE, this bird is a prime example of how well some birds can adapt to the human environment.

In wild situations, robins favour open broken woodland and forest clearings. They are equally at home in the city, manicured lawns replacing forest openings as feeding areas. They are natural inhabitants of our backyards, parks and golf courses, where ornamental trees and shrubs are much to their liking.

Recognized as the harbingers of spring — although other species do return earlier — the robin is also occasionally found here in the winter, in sheltered locations where there is an adequate supply of food.

Early in spring, robins can be seen running across the lawn in search of earthworms. They find burrowed worms by sight and not by sound, as is popularly believed. As the season progresses, robins devour huge amounts of berries.

Any ledge or building recess is a potential nest site, as are trees and shrubs. Four pastel blue-green eggs are laid.

Although well adapted to the urban environment, local populations could be adversely affected by excessive use of pesticides in gardens and parks, and domestic cats present a threat to nestlings.

GRAY CATBIRD
Dumetella carolinensis
Moqueur chat
smaller than robin-sized

THE GRAY CATBIRD is easily identified by its mostly slate-grey colour, black cap, and patch of chestnut under the tail. An inhabitant of dense thickets, vine tangles and the hedges and shrubs of city gardens, its attractive song is often heard from the top or from within the thicket. The song is a series of pleasant musical phrases, sometimes discordant, at other times imitating the songs of other birds. As well, a soft, unmistakable cat-like mewing is often used.

Most of its diet is comprised of insects like crickets, grasshoppers and June beetles, making it a valuable asset to the garden. Later in the summer, it eats many kinds of wild berries such as elderberry and wild grape.

The bulky nest is constructed one to three metres above the ground, a combination of twigs, grass and weed stems with the interior lined with fine rootlets and shreds of bark. The three to five unmarked, greenish-blue eggs are incubated by the female.

In the countryside surrounding Toronto, Gray Catbirds can be abundant in retired farmland and pasture where hawthorns and old apple trees are common.

Homeowners in such areas as the Niagara Escarpment and similar old farm sections, are almost sure to hear this vocal bird establishing its territory each spring.

BROWN THRASHER

Toxostoma rufum
Moqueur roux
robin-sized

BROWN THRASHERS ARE DISTINGUISHED by their bright reddish-brown upper parts and very heavily streaked breasts. They show a habitat preference for dense, thorny bushes, and retired, marginal farmlands with many hawthorns are good places to look for them. The Brown Thrasher tends to shun human habitation. Nevertheless, it is common during migration in the city's ravines and some will select these areas for breeding.

The nest is built in thick shrubbery, the thornier the better. The nest is low in the bush and is sometimes located directly on the ground. Loosely constructed of twigs, bark and grass, it is lined with fine rootlets. The four or five eggs are a pale bluish-white, covered with small brown dots.

The Brown Thrasher most often feeds on the ground, foraging among the fallen leaves and plant litter underneath shrubs and trees. It seldom scratches the ground with its feet, but uses its bill to toss the leaves aside in its search for grubs and beetles. It will jump from the ground to catch flying insects and eagerly devours ripe berries later in the season.

The loud song, often delivered from atop a bush or tree, is a series of musical notes with many phrases repeated in pairs, a characteristic that makes the bird easy to identify once the song becomes familiar.

CEDAR WAXWING

Bombycilla cedrorum
Jaseur des cèdres
larger than sparrow-sized

AT FIRST GLANCE, this species is similar to the Bohemian Waxwing, although it is a little smaller. Unlike its relative, the Cedar Waxwing is found throughout most of Ontario and is a common breeding bird in this area. The red, wax-like extensions of the secondary wing feathers give the bird its name.

The habitat of the Cedar Waxwing is extremely varied and includes residential areas and open woodlands to the tree-line. It is one of the later nesting birds, usually from late June through August. The bulky nest is built out on the branch of a tree or bush. Three to five eggs, pale-bluish grey with dots of black or brown, are laid.

Except during the breeding season when they pair off, waxwings spend most of their time in flocks. This is a good strategy: it confuses predators and gives the individual a better chance to get away. More importantly, however, many eyes are better than a single pair for detecting danger.

Cedar Waxwings devour many insects in summer and are therefore quite beneficial. They gorge themselves on berries, but their fondness for cherries may bring on the wrath of fruit growers.

EUROPEAN STARLING

Sturnus vulgaris
Étourneau sansonnet
smaller than robin-sized

A TRULY FAMILIAR BIRD in the city, the European Starling is with us year round. Introduced to New York in 1890 from Europe, starlings have shown a remarkable ability to adapt to their surroundings, and have spread rapidly from one end of the continent to the other.

The bird nests in tree cavities, crevices or openings in buildings or on old fence posts. In natural situations, the more aggressive starling can displace native birds from their nest sites.

Starlings can roost in huge numbers and more than one neighbourhood has been upset with the noise and mess when its trees were occupied for roosting. Starlings also do immense good, feeding on weed seeds and insects and grubs on lawns and in city parks. They also frequent bird feeders.

Terrific mimics, European Starlings incorporate parts of other bird songs into their own, as well as repeating a variety of the neighbourhood's squeaks and whistles.

WARBLING VIREO

Vireo gilvus

Viréo mélodieux

sparrow-sized

THIS DRAB, PALE GREY VIREO has no obvious field marks but does it sing! A treetop bird, the male sings continuously, filling the air with its song from its arrival in spring until late summer. Even on the hottest, most humid days its flowing warble can be heard.

An open woodland bird, the Warbling Vireo is at home in the mature shade trees of our parks and neighbourhoods. Where this habitat exists, the Warbling Vireo is usually present.

The nest is a well made cup suspended from the fork of a twig high up in the tree. Three to five eggs are laid which are incubated by both sexes. The nest is difficult to find as it is often obscured by the tree top leaves.

Warbling Vireos forage for insects in the tree canopy. Caterpillars, insect larvae, and other assorted bugs make up its diet. In late summer, they also feed on the abundant wild berries found on many shrubs throughout our area.

RED-EYED VIREO

Vireo olivaceus
Viréo aux yeux rouges
sparrow-sized

VIREOS ARE SMALL plain woodland birds that lack any conspicuous plumage pattern. They are dull greenish-olive on the upperparts and the term "vireo," derived from the Latin, refers to this drab colouration.

The Red-eyed Vireo is the only vireo with a red eye. The crown of its head is greyish, but over the eye there is a broad whitish stripe which is bordered on each side by a black line. The bird lacks wing bars.

Although dull-coloured and hard to distinguish in the field, it is one of our most common songbirds and inhabits almost every city park, ravine and wooded neighbourhood. The bird is a persistent singer, its song delivered tirelessly throughout the day, even on the hottest afternoons when other birds are silent.

The Red-eyed Vireo inhabits primarily broad-leaved trees and tall shrubbery. Here, in a slow deliberate pattern, it forages among the leaves for insects. It may be difficult to see among the leaves, but once you are familiar with its song you will detect it in woodlots everywhere.

Usually the nest is constructed about eye-level. It is a well made cup suspended by its edge in the fork of a branch. Many of the empty nests found in winter belong to this species.

YELLOW WARBLER

Dendroica petechia
Paruline jaune
smaller than sparrow-sized

THIS IS THE COMMON WARBLER throughout Canada, from southern Ontario to the limit of trees. The bright, colourful songster is often called a wild canary, and is the most likely warbler to be seen in the city.

Easily identified by sight, the male has reddish breast streaks. The streaks are faint or absent in the female and overall, she is a paler colour. Watch for the yellow tail spots in both sexes. As its name suggests, this bird is yellow throughout.

A symbol of spring, most return in early May but some individuals can be seen in late April. The males start singing as soon as they arrive to establish their territories. It is then that these birds are easiest to spot, before all the trees and shrubs are in full leaf. They live in the shrubbery of gardens and along the edges of ponds and streams, avoiding densely wooded areas.

The nest is fastened to a fork of a branch and is made of grasses and other similar materials. The nest is often parasitized by the Brown-headed Cowbird which lays one of its eggs in the nest. Depending on the time of the egg laying, the warbler may abandon the nest, build a second storey over the existing nest or incubate and raise the cowbird as its own, usually to the detriment of warbler young.

YELLOW-RUMPED WARBLER

Dendroica coronata
Paruline à croupion jaune
smaller than sparrow-sized

OF ALL THE COLOURFUL SONGBIRDS that appear in spring in our gardens and ravines, the Yellow-rumped Warbler is one of the most numerous. It is the earliest warbler to arrive, usually in late April, and is the last warbler species to depart in autumn. On rare occasions, an individual may even overwinter, subsisting on berries and seeds; unusual for a species which is primarily an insect eater.

The Yellow-rumped Warbler is widespread as a breeding bird in Ontario, preferring coniferous woodlands. It adapts readily to areas disturbed by power lines, fire or logging as it likes to inhabit the edges of forest openings. In breeding season, it is more common from the edge of the Canadian Shield north; however, it is found in agricultural Ontario where remnant coniferous habitats still exist.

The nest is built in a coniferous tree, of twigs, grass and similar material. The inside is lined with feathers and hair. Generally four to five white eggs with grey and brown specks are laid with incubation being done by the female.

Yellow-rumped Warblers have one of the most extensive distribution ranges in Canada, being found from the Atlantic coast to the Pacific, and as far north as the Mackenzie River Delta.

BLACK-AND-WHITE WARBLER

Mniotilta varia
Paruline noir et blanc
smaller than sparrow-sized

THIS BIRD IS BOLDLY STRIPED in black and white except on the belly which is pure white. It creeps along branches and trunks of trees, a distinctive habit which distinguishes it from other warblers.

Widespread in Ontario, it is among the four or five early species of warbler to return in the spring. It is a quiet bird and unlike some other warbler species it can be inconspicuous. The song is a high-pitched, thin *weesee, weesee, weesee, weesee,* and you have to look to find its owner.

Like so many other species in spring, city ravines and older neighbourhoods with lots of trees are excellent areas to find this species. During migration, a ravine can be alive with birds one day and virtually empty the next. Some of the less-manicured conservation areas in the region also offer this bird good habitat.

The Black-and-white Warbler breeds in deciduous or mixed woodlands, often in moist situations with cedar swamps being especially attractive. The nest is built on the ground, often at the base of a tree or stump. Five eggs are usually laid in the well concealed nest.

AMERICAN REDSTART
Setophaga ruticilla
Paruline flamboyante
smaller than sparrow-sized

ITS SHOWY HALLOWEEN COLOURS and constant activity make this flashy warbler immediately recognizable: a spectacular "butterfly" of the bird world. Rarely still, the American Redstart flits from bush to bush, snatching up insects from the twigs and leaves and darting out to catch insects on the wing.

Redstarts are inhabitants of the deciduous woodlands, frequenting the shrubby understory. Common summer residents in our region, they are often seen in wooded areas and back yards in the city and surrounding countryside. They are particularly common in cottage country, where the second growth woodlands are much to their liking. Their constant activity, bright colour, and ability to live in small wooded areas make American Redstarts highly noticeable, even to the casual observer.

The startling orange and black colour and white underparts of the male American Redstart are not acquired until the bird's second year. The female has yellow patches in place of the male's orange, and a greyish head blending into olive on the back.

The well built nest is settled in an upright crotch of a young tree or in a large shrub. The cup-shaped nest contains about four whitish, brown-spotted eggs which are incubated by the female. Redstarts have a high-pitched, variable song. Once you have learned one song, listen for different renditions of it.

OVENBIRD

Seiurus aurocapillus
Paruline couronnée
sparrow-sized

YOU WILL HEAR THIS BIRD more often than you will see it. Its loud repetitive song, *teacher-teacher-teacher*, is easily recognized and for a brief few days in May, it reverberates throughout our wooded river valleys and ravines. After this interlude, Ovenbirds are rarely found in urban areas, although many a holiday in cottage country is accompanied by their song — even on hot afternoons, when most other songbirds are silent.

Ovenbirds are typically inhabitants of older deciduous and mixed forests, where the tree canopy obscures the sky and there is little shrubby understory but a lot of leaf litter. They are usually seen walking on the ground or on low branches. Their olive-green upperparts allow these large warblers to blend into the forest floor, and they will rarely flush in the woods unless the human intruder is virtually upon them.

The nest is built on the ground, often in more open areas of the forest. It is constructed in the form of an arch with the opening in front, giving it the appearance of an oven. The dead-leaf roof conceals the nest and shields it from the rain. As a ground nester, the Ovenbird is subject to much predation from snakes, squirrels and skunks and other animals that forage on the forest floor.

COMMON YELLOWTHROAT

Geothlypis trichas
Paruline masquée
smaller than sparrow-sized

ONE OF THE MOST ABUNDANT of all warblers, the male Common Yellowthroat, with its jet black facial marks and bright yellow throat, is unmistakable. Yellowthroats use a variety of habitats including edges of streams, bogs, low bushes and thickets, but in our region it is most often found in the cattail marshes of the river valleys surrounding the city.

The song — *witchity, witchity, witchity, witchity* — is loud, and can be identified without too much difficulty. In breeding season, the male can be seen singing from a prominent perch, such as a cattail or shrub.

Usually the birds carry out most of their activities in the lower levels of vegetation; consequently, they can be frustratingly difficult to see. Yellowthroats are extremely active birds, almost wren-like in their energy.

The nest is constructed on the ground or slightly above. Made of weed stalks, grasses, sedges and other material it seems rather bulky. Usually four eggs are laid which are incubated by the female for about twelve days. When the young hatch, both parents can be commonly seen carrying insects to the nest.

91

NORTHERN CARDINAL

Cardinalis cardinalis
Cardinal rouge
smaller than robin-sized

ONE OF THE BEST KNOWN BIRDS of our area, the Northern Cardinal frequents our neighbourhoods and ravines year-round. In early spring, the loud songs of both sexes vibrate throughout this area, and in winter the plumage of the male presents a vivid image against the snow.

The Northern Cardinal is a relative newcomer from the United States. The first nest in Ontario was found at Point Pelee in 1901. Since then, the cardinal has moved northward to become common in Toronto and throughout southwestern Ontario, and is now found frequently in the Ottawa region as well.

The Northern Cardinal is one bird which has profited from urbanization. Land clearing created many edge habitats between fields and woodlots, a favoured nesting site. The new shrubs and small trees planted in towns and cities provided appropriate vegetation. This habitat together with the proliferation of bird feeders has provided ideal conditions for this bird's expansion in distribution.

The bowl-shaped nest, loosely constructed by the female, is made of twigs, bark and grasses and is built in tangles in tall shrubbery, small conifers or decidu-ous trees. Three or four gre-yish- or greenish-white eggs, spotted or blotched with brown, are laid.

Cardinals eat a variety of insects and wild fruit is also relished, as are buds and blossoms. At feeding stations, sun-flower seeds and cracked corn are popular.

ROSE-BREASTED GROSBEAK

Pheucticus ludovicianus
Cardinal à poitrine rose
smaller than robin-sized

THE ROSE-BREASTED GROSBEAK is a common, popular songbird wherever second growth and mature broad-leaved woodlands are found. It is seen along edges of woodlands, pastures, borders of streams and in the wooded parks, ravines and other treed areas of Toronto.

Its arrival in May is heralded by a melodic continuous song, similar to a Robin's but more forceful, rapid and richer in tone. Because of its constant song, we can easily spot the tropical-like beauty of the male. The female is much duller, being a dark buffy brown with brown-streaked white underparts.

Rose-breasted Grosbeaks forage in trees, feeding on insects, buds, blossoms and fruit. Their number has increased in recent years, probably because of the regrowth of forests in settled areas and their ability to nest successfully even in small woodlots.

Male grosbeaks sometimes select the nest site, which is always located in deciduous greenery, and may help the female construct the nest. Usually located at a relatively low level, nests have been seen as high up as eight to sixteen metres.

The four eggs, of variable colouration are incubated by both parents for twelve to thirteen days.

The Rose-breasted Grosbeak becomes scarce by the end of September as it has departed for the wintering grounds in southern Mexico or northern South America.

93

INDIGO BUNTING

Passerina cyanea
Passerin indigo
sparrow-sized

COMMON SUMMER RESIDENTS of the valleys and shrubby fields within our region, male Indigo Buntings sing conspicuously from high perches such as utility wires and exposed branches. This behaviour constitutes an aggressive defense of territory against other males.

The species prefers an area of bushy ground-cover for nest sites, and trees along the woodland edge for singing. Abandoned farms and pastures where second growth occurs are favourite habitats. Buntings are also common along roadsides and utility rights-of-way.

The origin of the name "bunting" is unknown. The scientific name, "cyanea," means dark blue, an excellent description of the male, which is is one of the most handsome songbirds in Ontario. The female is a rather nondescript brown.

The breeding range for Indigo Buntings in Ontario is restricted to deciduous and mixed wood forest. The nest is a cup-like structure not far from the ground, often within raspberry or equally impenetrable bushes. The female incubates three to four blue-white eggs for twelve to thirteen days and about ten days after hatching the young leave the nest.

Buntings forage in trees, shrubbery and on the ground for a variety of foods from grasshoppers and beetles to the seeds of dandelion, thistle, aster and goldenrod. In winter, they migrate to the Caribbean and Central America.

AMERICAN TREE SPARROW

Spizella arborea
Bruant hudsonien
sparrow-sized

WHEN THE WINDS OF AUTUMN remind us that winter is just around the corner, American Tree Sparrows begin to make their appearance, en route from the far north. In small flocks, they move about in the backyard shrubbery or roadside wooded edges, rummaging for the seeds of weeds or roadside flowers.

Tree Sparrows are distinguished by a brown blotch in the middle of a clear, grey breast. Two white wing-bars are prominent as is the rusty brown cap.

The bird nests along the tree-line areas of Ontario where there are shrubs like willow and dwarf birch. The nest can be on the ground or located in one of the low shrubs. On the breeding grounds, it has a wonderful, melodious song.

Known in our region only as a winter bird, Tree Sparrows are regular visitors to bird feeders. They are also commonly seen in weedy, uncultivated fields or along roadsides and hedgerows that provide a good supply of seed.

CHIPPING SPARROW

Spizella passerina
Bruant familier
smaller than sparrow-sized

THE CHIPPING SPARROW can be found in openings and edges of woodlands, scattered trees, orchards, gardens, and lawns. It has adapted so well to human environments that it is one of the most abundant species in Ontario, and it is often one of the first to pioneer new subdivisions.

The bird gets its name from its chipping call notes. One of our smallest and tamest sparrows, it can be easily recognized by its rust or chestnut cap, and the distinct white line above the eye. In autumn, the colours are much duller.

The female builds the nest and from grass and weed stems, lined with finer material such as hair. The nest is usually up to two metres above the ground and located in an evergreen. Four light blue, spotted eggs are incubated by the female for eleven to thirteen days.

Chipping Sparrows eat insects and large amounts of weed seeds from our lawns, including crabgrass and dandelion. Chipping Sparrows are found in the Toronto area until late October, when most have left for the warmer climates of the southern and central United States.

FIELD SPARROW

Spizella pusilla
Bruant des champs
sparrow-sized

THE FIELD SPARROW has an unstreaked breast, pink bill, rusty cap and upperparts. Its song is quite pleasing and distinctive.

Abandoned farmlands, overgrown pastures and areas awaiting development around the city, are typical habitats for this bird. In more rural areas, marginal farmland with hedgerows, trees and bushes often provides ideal habitat. Extensive cultivation of farmland, however, has eliminated much habitat suitable for the bird.

The male defends his territory against other males by flying to various trees and shrubs, announcing his presence with a sweet, whistled song. The nest is on or near the ground, either in the grass or in small shrubs, where the female incubates the three to five eggs. Cowbirds frequently lay their eggs in the nests of Field Sparrows, and the larger cowbird young monopolize the food and displace the nestling sparrows.

SAVANNAH SPARROW

Passerculus sandwichensis
Bruant des prés
smaller than sparrow-sized

AN INHABITANT OF OPEN GRASSLANDS — meadows, pastures, hayfields and just about every other open grassy area — the Savannah Sparrow is one of the most widely distributed birds in Canada. It is found from the Arctic to the hydro rights-of-way in southern Ontario cities.

A nondescript streaked sparrow, it has a short yellow line above the eye. The Savannah Sparrow is a persistent singer, using fences, wires, and tall plants from which to deliver its song.

The nest is well concealed on the ground in a natural hollow or in one made by the bird. The nest is lined with grass and is often sheltered by a shrub or small tree. Four to six whitish eggs, variably splashed with brown, are laid. The female incubates the eggs for about twelve days.

As Savannah Sparrows eat large quantities of weed seeds, they are very beneficial birds in rural areas.

Top: Savannah Sparrow
Middle: White-throated Sparrow
Bottom: Song Sparrow

SONG SPARROW

Melospiza melodia
Bruant chanteur
sparrow-sized

AN EARLY AND WELCOME spring arrival, the Song Sparrow can begin nesting as early as mid-April. This species is common in thickets, along the margins of ponds, streams and rivers and in bushy hedgerows. It is also a resident of treed neighbourhoods.

Most nests are built on the ground especially early in the season. In southern Ontario, two or three broods can be produced in a season. Generally, three to five eggs are laid.

Insects comprise much of the Song Sparrow's food in summer but as the season progresses, it will eat the fruit of many shrubs. Song Sparrows will also visit bird feeders.

WHITE-THROATED SPARROW

Zonotrichia albicollis
Bruant à gorge blanche
sparrow-sized

THIS CHUNKY SPARROW with its striped head and well defined white throat patch is an abundant migrant through our region. Ravines, brush piles, back yard shrubbery and wooded parks can be virtually alive with this species in spring. Its song — variously described as *Sam Peabody, Peabody, Peabody* and *I-love-Canada, Canada, Canada,* — vibrates through the wooded residential areas, bringing cheer in spring.

White-throated Sparrows are quite widespread. Those of us who have spent any time in cottage country or in places like Algonquin Park are as familiar with this species as a symbol of Ontario's wild as we are with the Common Loon.

Residents of bushy openings, cutover areas and the edges of mixed wood forests, White-throats build their nests on or near the ground in thickets. Generally, four eggs are laid.

Occasionally, an individual may remain in our region during the winter months.

DARK-EYED JUNCO

Junco hyemalis
Junco ardoisé
sparrow-sized

ADULT JUNCOS are easily-recognized sparrows, the distinctive grey hood, sharply separated from the white underparts and white outer tail feathers, being diagnostic.

Very common migrants in our region in April and late fall, many Dark-eyed Juncos remain in winter to add considerable interest at our feeders. In the nesting season, they are primarily inhabitants of the mixed forest area of the Canadian Shield, and prefer woodland edges and forest openings to the deep forest. The species appears to like burned-over areas, and its trilling song is commonplace throughout the lake and cottage country of the province.

The nest is usually on the ground in forest openings, well hidden in the shelter of a tree or stump. Four to five eggs are laid in the cup-shaped nest. Young juncos leave the nest when they are about thirteen days old.

Watch for the species during migration in your back yard, and in river valleys, ravines and similar wooded habitats.

BOBOLINK

Dolichonyx oryzivorus
Goglu
smaller than robin-sized

BOBOLINKS MIGRATE NORTHWARD each spring from southern Brazil and northern Argentina to the grasslands of southern Canada. Their migration flight is the longest undertaken by a member of the blackbird family. The male Bobolinks arrive several days ahead of the females, filling the air with their tinkling, bubbling songs as they engage in aerial displays.

The male is strikingly handsome, coloured in black, white and yellowish-buff. The females on the other hand are somewhat nondescript, an excellent adaption for a bird that nests on the ground.

Bobolinks are residents of open fields containing taller grasses, clover and wildflowers, and in agricultural fields containing alfalfa. The bird is common in agricultural Ontario and can be readily seen from May to August in the open fields surrounding the city.

In summer, large quantities of beetles, grasshoppers and other insects as well as grass seeds are eaten. In the early part of this century, the birds were killed in great numbers in the southern United States because of the damage they inflicted on rice crops.

101

RED-WINGED BLACKBIRD

Agelaius phoeniceus
Carouge à épaulettes
smaller than robin-sized

THE GURGLING *KONK-A-REE* song of the Red-winged Blackbird announces the advent of spring. The males are hard to misidentify, perched on cattails displaying their bright red wing patches in all their sexual splendour.

Red-winged Blackbirds are residents of marshes and water edges filled with cattails. They often nest in loose colonies with their rough grass nests built over water on two or more cattail stalks. Usually four eggs are laid, and are incubated by the female. The colonies can be noisy, with the calls of the males being used frequently to resolve territorial disputes.

The Red-winged Blackbird has adapted to pasture lands and roadsides. It roosts in large numbers, with huge flocks blackening the sky as the birds leave their chosen roosting area in the marsh. After nesting, the birds are found everywhere. In autumn, they feed on waste grain that has been left in the agricultural fields but at certain times during the growing season, they can cause damage to standing corn. In spring and summer, they eat insects and weed seeds.

During the summer, look for Red-winged Blackbirds in any wetland around the city.

EASTERN MEADOWLARK

Sturnella magna
Sturnelle des prés
robin-sized

EASTERN MEADOWLARKS are birds of open, grassy areas, occupying the fields, meadows and pastures which surround our region. Within the city itself, weedy areas, utility rights-of-way and similar open spaces often contain a pair or two. Despite the common name, the bird is not a lark but a member of the blackbird family. It was likely named for its melodious spring song, which has been welcomed by generations of rural dwellers.

A brownish bird, with a rich lemon-yellow breast handsomely marked with a black V, it delivers its clear song from fence posts, utility poles and wires.

The males return first, in April, followed by the females a week or so later. Resident males then begin to sing, proclaiming territory. Some males may have more than one mate.

The nest, concealed in the grass, often has a dome-shaped roof. Five eggs are commonly laid. The eggs are incubated by the female, but both parents feed the young.

Eastern Meadowlarks are voracious eaters of a variety of insects.

COMMON GRACKLE

Quiscalus quiscula
Quiscale bronzé
robin-sized

COMMON GRACKLES APPEAR in early spring. Very common in our region, they often gather in flocks and frequently mix with Red-winged Blackbirds, starlings and Brown-headed Cowbirds. They appear to be black, but a close look will reveal a surprisingly handsome iridescent plumage of blue, purple and bronze. The tail is long and wedge-shaped.

Easily satisfied in their habitat requirements, grackles can be found on lawns, golf courses, in marshes, parks or wet woodlands. The broad habitat use displayed by the species is also reflected in its wide-ranging diet. Weed seeds, waste grain, insects, garbage, as well as the young nestlings and eggs of other species, keep the bird well fed.

Highly gregarious, Common Grackles can roost at night in huge numbers. Although individual nests are found, grackles will nest in small colonies as well. The bulky nest is built of sticks and weeds and is plastered together with mud. Grackles frequently select conifers for nesting but as the habitat description suggests, the nest may be constructed in a variety of situations.

BROWN-HEADED COWBIRD

Molothrus ater
Vacher à tête brune
sparrow-sized

THE MALE COWBIRD with its coffee-brown head and black body is easy to recognize at close range, while the female is a nondescript brownish-grey. Widespread in agricultural and residential areas, the bird forages in open grassy areas or cultivated fields where it can eat many insects and weed seeds. The name is derived from its practice of feeding on the insects kicked up by cattle.

Famous or notorious for its parasitic habits, depending on your point of view, cowbirds build no nests. Instead, the female lays its eggs in the nests of other small birds, such as Yellow Warblers and Chipping Sparrows. She lays only one egg in each nest, although another cowbird may select the same nest later. There is some evidence that indicates a female cowbird can lay up to ten or twelve eggs each season.

The host bird may push the cowbird egg from the nest, but most often it incubates the egg along with its own. Cowbirds hatch first, and develop rapidly. Their persistent begging, fast growth and aggressive behaviour deprive the host's young of food, and they may starve to death. Sometimes young cowbirds will push the host's young from the nest. The host bird will continue to feed the young cowbird, oblivious to the fact that it is a different species.

NORTHERN ORIOLE
Icterus galbula
Oriole du Nord
smaller than robin-sized

THE NORTHERN ORIOLE is one of the most striking birds to be seen in our region. The vivid gold-orange underparts contrasted with the solid black head leaves little room for misidentification. The female is less vividly coloured, being olive above and a dull yellow-orange below.

A resident of the upper parts of tall deciduous trees, the Northern Oriole is often obscured by the foliage, but its loud, distinct, melodious song gives the bird away. The male is a frequent singer in May; once paired, he sings much less often.

The nest is not too difficult to find as it is an obvious bag-like structure suspended from a tree branch, carefully woven with various plant fibres. The entrance to this hanging structure is from the top. In autumn, when the leaves have fallen, the used nests are easily sighted, and old nests may persist for several years.

Northern Orioles consume a variety of insects and are one of the few species that will eat tent caterpillars.

Look for the bird along woodland edges, open wooded roadsides, and in parks and neighbourhoods where tall shade trees are found.

HOUSE FINCH
Carpodacus mexicanus
Roselin familier
smaller than sparrow-sized

THE HOUSE FINCH IS A RECENT ARRIVAL to this area. Breeding evidence for the bird was not obtained in Ontario until 1978 but since that time, the population has expanded rapidly.

It is now a common species in southern Ontario, especially in urban centres where a variety of nesting sites are provided.

The House Finch nests in ornamental bushes and shrubs, evergreens, buildings or bird boxes. Four to five speckled, blue-white eggs are laid in the nest which is usually two or three metres above the ground. Two broods are raised during the long nesting season.

The male House Finch is a conspicuous songster. Its bright red crown, heart and rump and striped flanks distinguish it from the dark raspberry jam-coloured Purple Finch, with which it is easily confused. House Finches now greatly outnumber Purple Finches in this area.

The House Finch is very adaptable to the human environment, a characteristic shared with the House Sparrow. In southwestern North America, the species occupies a niche similar to that of the House Sparrow, and as it spreads in our area, it occupies the same habitat.

COMMON REDPOLL

Carduelis flammea

Sizerin flammé

smaller than sparrow-sized

ANOTHER WINTER FINCH, the Common Redpoll breeds only in far northern latitudes: in Ontario, the barrenlands and shrub-tundra areas of the Hudson Bay lowlands are favoured.

This irruptive species may be found in our area in large numbers one winter, and not seen at all the next. When present, immense flocks will move restlessly over weedy fields, devouring the seed heads projecting above the snow. Redpolls are also fond of birch and alder seeds.

Individual birds will come to bird feeders for millet and the smaller black variety of sunflower seeds.

Redpolls are brownish, streaked birds with a red cap, black chin and pink on the breast. Watch for their twittering flocks in weedy fields or old bushy hedgerows.

On the tundra breeding grounds, Redpolls construct their nests in small shrubs, one of the few far northern nesting birds to build them above the ground.

PINE SISKIN
Carduelis pinus
Chardonneret des pins
smaller than sparrow-sized

THIS SMALL, HEAVILY STREAKED, brownish bird can be a delight around the bird feeder. The yellow in the wing and tail is not very noticeable when the bird is perching, but is immediately visible when it takes flight.

The presence of Pine Siskins in this region is variable: they can be very common one year and virtually absent in the same area the next. In winters of high abundance, a few may remain to nest. The species tends to be gregarious, and even during the nest season, the bird can be found in small flocks.

The Pine Siskin prefers a habitat of mixed coniferous and deciduous trees, but it will use ornamental bushes and shade tree areas for nesting. The nest, a cup of fine twigs and rootlets, is usually in a conifer. Three to five pale blue eggs are laid, beginning in very early spring.

Pine Siskins eat the seeds of conifers, birch and dandelions, as well as small buds and insects.

AMERICAN GOLDFINCH

Carduelis tristis
Chardonneret jaune
smaller than sparrow-sized

THE "WILD CANARY" of the countryside, American Goldfinches are common throughout southern Ontario. The bright yellow colouration of the male, with its black cap, wings and tail, is unmistakable. The female is more drab — brownish-olive tinged with yellow, and with no black cap. The adults in winter are mainly brownish-olive.

Goldfinches are often seen in flocks. Their obvious undulating flight is a characteristic field mark.

Goldfinches do not begin nesting until well into July, later than most other birds. It is believed that late nesting is the bird's adaptation to the occurrence of summer seeds of plants such as the thistle, upon which young goldfinches are fed.

Old pastures with small shrubs and hawthorns are good places to find the bird. Goldfinches are also seen in residential areas, where they visit gardens to feed on the seeds of cosmos, zinnias and other domestic plants. They will also visit the feeder in winter, where they enjoy the smaller variety of sunflower seeds.

EVENING GROSBEAK

Coccothraustes vespertinus
Gros-bec errant
smaller than robin-sized

COMMONLY SEEN IN WINTER, Evening Grosbeaks will feed on maple and ash keys, small crabapples and mountain ash berries. Grosbeaks are well known for descending upon bird feeders in urban areas, where they gorge themselves on sunflower seeds. Their arrival at the bird feeder can be exciting, as they are resplendent against the snow, although their presence may wear a little thin with time, given their ravenous appetites.

The black, white and yellow plumage of the adult male is elegant; the adult female is mostly greyish, tinged with greenish-yellow. The Evening Grosbeak is a plump bird with a distinctive, undulating flight pattern. Large white wing patches are very noticeable in flight.

Its breeding habitat is primarily the coniferous and mixed wood areas of the province, where it will nest in either a conifer or deciduous tree.

The bird wanders widely after nesting. In the Toronto area, it is usually found only in the winter months. In some winters it may be scarce here, depending upon the availability of adequate food supplies farther north.

HOUSE SPARROW
Passer domesticus
Moineau domestique
sparrow-sized

THE COMMON HOUSE SPARROW is a stocky, noisy bird with a black throat and bib and chestnut markings. The female is duller and unmarked, and can easily be confused with other species of sparrow. The song is a monotonous series of chirps.

Sparrows are often found in flocks, as those of us who operate feeding stations will readily attest. They survive with no difficulty wherever there is human settlement — from the city core to the rural barn. Not native to North America, the bird has rapidly adapted to the New World after its introduction in the nineteenth century, obtaining the status of a pest in many areas.

Voracious eaters, House Sparrows respond quickly to breadcrumbs or picnic leftovers, and they will quickly make a mess of the bird feed-tray.

House Sparrows will nest anywhere, and will frequently take over nest boxes set out to attract other species. Most often five eggs are laid.

Although their practice of feeding on human garbage has its benefits, the proliferation of House Sparrows on this continent is an example of the liabilities involved with introducing species to new environments.

ATTRACTING BIRDS

GETTING STARTED at birdwatching need not cost a lot of money. Many people derive a great deal of pleasure by simply putting out household scraps for birds on a homemade feeder, close enough to the window that birds can be seen as they come and go.

It is certainly not necessary to be able to identify all the birds at the feeder to be able to enjoy them, but there is a great sense of satisfaction in being able to tell one species from another. Human nature being what it is, we tend to want to learn.

Most people interested in watching birds use binoculars, as this allows them to identify key characteristics such as plumage, leg colour, and bill shape. Binoculars also allow the user to watch the more timid birds that normally stay at a distance, or remain in the cover of bushes and trees, and they allow us to study birds' behaviour. Small details help to build the overall picture of a bird, which helps to identify the species.

Buying binoculars is perhaps the biggest financial outlay the birdwatcher will make, but it is not necessary to spend a great deal of money as there are many inexpensive but good models. Buying

An attractive back yard offers many birdwatching opportunities.

114

binoculars can be confusing, and much has been written about how to choose a pair. The best advice is to ask a birdwatcher or to talk to someone at a local nature centre. Remember that no one pair will be perfect for every situation — watching birds in woodland requires binoculars with a wide field of view but a reasonably low magnification (8X would be ideal), whereas watching shorebirds in an estuary would require a higher magnification, and a telescope would then be useful. Binoculars tend to get heavy around the neck, and it is a good idea to keep this in mind when selecting the right pair. A wider neck strap certainly helps, but if you have a choice, you will not regret going for the lightest pair that seems to be right for you.

Aside from binoculars, the only other piece of equipment needed is a book that will enable you to identify the birds you see. Armed with a pair of binoculars and a good field guide, you will find a whole new world opening up for you as you take advantage of the many excellent birdwatching sites in and around the city, or enjoy your own back yard birds more.

Soon, you will be taking your binoculars with you on a hike or as you take the dog for a walk in the park — the opportunities for their use are endless.

Birds are easily viewed in their natural habitat through binoculars.

BIRD FEEDERS

Why bother with a bird feeder in your back yard? The great advantage is that by feeding birds on a regular basis, they learn to come to that spot every day and as more birds learn, the numbers of species and individuals increase. Your back yard can become your own bird sanctuary.

Feeders also provide advantages for birds. They are used much more frequently when natural food sources are less abundant—particularly in the winter months. When the weather gets colder, the birds using the neighbourhood feeders may rely on this food source for survival. Late autumn is a good time to establish feeders, as this is when birds are setting up their winter territories.

Once feeding is started, it should be maintained throughout the winter and particularly during the colder weather. A break in the normal routine could well mean that the birds you have so carefully attracted will move on. Try feeding the birds at the same time each day and you will notice how they quickly adjust to a daily routine. Early morning is best. Better still, provide sufficient food to last two or three days.

There may only be a few birds at the feeder at any one time, but this does not necessarily mean that only a few birds are using the feeder. It can be difficult to recognize individuals, but by banding

Blue Jays at a tray feeder.

Black-capped Chickadees at a seed dispenser.

and watching them as they come back to feeders, it has been shown that birds use feeders for only short periods during the day. Any one feeder may be visited by many individuals throughout the daylight hours as they forage through the neighbourhood. This is normal, particularly in the winter when they must range over a much wider area to find the variety of foods they need to sustain themselves.

When you place a feeder in the garden, don't expect the birds to find it immediately. It often takes a few weeks for numbers to build up, so persevere and be patient.

It is best to position the feeder some distance from the house, as the birds will be wary if they see movement. Find a site that is likely to be attractive to birds: immediately adjacent to dense trees or bushes for instance, rather than in the centre of the lawn. Immediate escape cover is as important as the food itself. Small birds are innately aware of the danger of avian predators such as hawks, and will soon take a liking to a feeder that offers safety as well as good fare.

Bear in mind also that cats can be a real threat, so make it difficult for them by ensuring that the birds have a chance to see them. Avoid positioning your feeder right beside a suitable hiding place, such as a low bush, and make sure that it is high enough to be out of reach of the agile cat — which can leap as high as two metres. A large circle of page wire under the feeder will soon dissuade the neighbour's Tabby.

There are countless designs for bird feeders, but essentially they all do exactly the same job: they dispense food for birds in a convenient and hygienic manner. Depending on the type of birds one wishes to attract, there are four basic designs:

- hanging seed dispensers
- tray feeders for mixed bird foods
- suet feeders
- hummingbird feeders

Hanging Seed Dispensers

These come in many different designs, but if you bear a few points in mind it is easy to select the right one.

The feeder should be large enough to hold a good supply of seeds; otherwise, you will be forever refilling it. The ease with which the feeder can be filled is also important. Birds will eat most during the coldest periods, so you'll need a feeder that is easy to open and close on a cold day when you're wearing gloves.

All feeders should be cleaned regularly so they should be easy to take apart. The seed should be protected from the rain and snow. Clear plastic seed containers are the most convenient—they

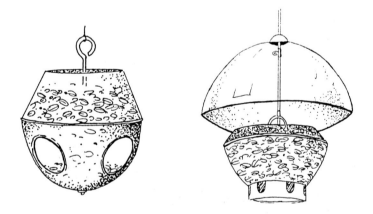

LEFT: A large seed dispenser that holds more food and has larger openings to allow bigger birds to use it.
RIGHT: A seed hopper with a plastic dome that keeps off squirrels and larger birds. It has good seed capability and is ideal for smaller birds.

clean easily, are reasonably strong, allow you to see when they need refilling, and allow the birds to see what is inside them.

There are many commercial seed mixtures available for hanging feeders, but a surprising number of birds seem to prefer sunflower seeds. It is a favorite food of Evening Grosbeaks, Blue Jays, Black-capped Chickadees and Northern Cardinals, among others. There are two types of sunflower seeds, the larger, striped variety and the smaller black one. Many winter finches prefer the latter.

Cracked corn is enjoyed by many species and is inexpensive compared to other foods. The "wild bird seed" mixtures will attract a number of birds, mainly House Sparrows. If you really want to please a Blue Jay, put out peanuts.

Tray Feeders

This type of feeder can be designed to attract many different types of birds, from seed eaters to those that forage on the ground. Some tray feeders have a hopper, with the tray immediately below to catch the seed and provide a feeding area. These work well, but have some disadvantages. There is never enough room for all the birds to feed without overcrowding, and so the more dominant species and individuals tend to drive others away. It is also quite difficult to see the birds at the feeder. The more timid ones tend to feed on the side furthest from your sight — a problem which can be overcome if you arrange to have only one outlet.

A tray-type feeder with a hopper that has a see-through side for easy checking of food levels.

119

Perhaps the best types of tray feeders are those that are nothing more than a large tray, onto which seed and other scraps are spread. It should have a lip to stop too much food from spilling or blowing onto the ground. But don't worry about the spillage; you will find that many species prefer to feed on the ground under the feeder. Position this type of feeder near some dense tree or shrub cover. And again, a temporary wire fence with at least 10 cm mesh will keep the cat from lunging directly under the feeder, yet will allow casual access for large birds.

Suet Feeders

You can get beef suet from the meat counter at the supermarket and birds such as woodpeckers and chickadees love it. It is a good high-energy food for birds in cold weather and is easy to maintain as it comes in a lump, lasts a while, and can be simply suspended in an old onion bag or from a string. Other types of suet feeders can be made: if you have the tools, bore holes in a short log and push suet into the holes, then hang this up.

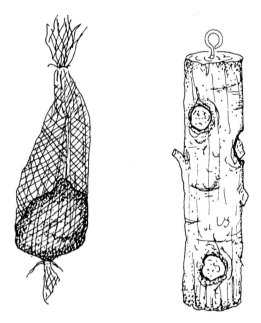

LEFT: *The simplest of all suet dispensers: an old onion bag, easily replaceable.*
RIGHT: *A more natural type of suet dispenser: an old log with holes drilled in it and stuffed with suet.*

Hummingbird Feeders

It is possible to attract hummingbirds into your garden with a colourful variety of flowers, but a good hummingbird feeder is one of the best ways to keep them coming back. When buying a feeder, look closely at the seals that keep the fluid in the container and choose one that looks well made. Most of them work, but the cheaper ones don't last long and frequently drip. This attracts wasps, bees and ants and leaves the feeder empty in short order. A hummingbird feeder should have some red on it, as this helps to attract the birds. You can make your own feeding fluid by dissolving two to three parts of white sugar in one to three parts of near-boiling water. Experiment and see what concentration seems to be preferred. There is no need to add red dye to the liquid, and never use honey as this ferments readily and may grow a mold that can be fatal to hummingbirds. It is important to clean the feeder frequently. In warm weather, add only a bit of liquid each time and let your feathered visitors consume it before it ferments. Keep the refill jar in the refrigerator.

Because hummingbirds are so small, it is most rewarding to hang the feeder near a window, or on the deck, where the birds quickly become accustomed to people and will allow you to watch at close range.

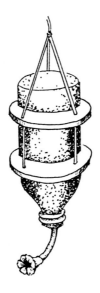

A home-made hummingbird feeder. Use an artificial red flower at the mouth.

NEST BOXES

Different species of birds have evolved to take advantage of different habitats. Each species uses a different feeding strategy and a different nesting strategy. By providing a variety of different types of food at your feeder, it is possible to attract ground-feeding birds and tree-feeding birds, seed eaters, omnivorous birds and even the odd bird of prey. The same is true if one provides a variety of different nesting opportunities. Birds will be attracted to artificial sites during the breeding season. Although some boxes may not be used the first year, they can be relocated next season.

There are many misconceptions about nest boxes. For example, birds don't need a perch on the front of the bird house — a perch is most useful for predators such as starlings that are trying to steal eggs or young. Although you may appreciate rounded corners on a bird house and a well-sanded exterior, birds prefer rough wood and a natural look. At the end of the season, clean the nest box out.

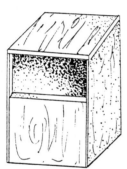

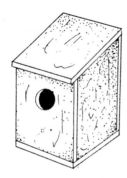

Different styles of nest boxes.

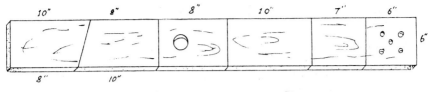

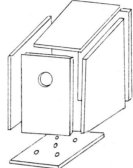

The construction of a nest box from a plank of wood.

This helps to prevent nest parasites from over-wintering, and gives birds a vacant box for the following spring. Don't disturb the house when it's in use as you may cause the adults to desert their eggs or young.

There are many different designs for nest boxes, but the most common and often the most effective is a very simple box that can be made from a single plank of wood. By altering the inside dimensions, the size of the hole, and the site where the box is placed, you should be able to attract a variety of different species.

Here are a few basic dimensions for some of the most common cavity nesting species:

Species	Floor Size	Depth	Hole Diameter	Height Above Ground
House Wren	10 x 10 cm	15 - 20 cm	2.5 cm	1 - 3 m
Black-capped Chickadee	10 x 10 cm	20 - 25 cm	3 cm	1.5 - 4.5 m
Tree Swallow	12 x 12 cm	15 - 25 cm	4 cm	1.5 - 4.5 m
Northern Flicker	20 x 20 cm	40 - 45 cm	7 cm	2.5 - 6 m

There are some basic rules to be kept in mind. If the nest box is exposed to full sunlight during the hottest part of the day, the nestlings may die from heat exhaustion, so choose a shaded area, or the sheltered side of an exposed tree, post or building. If the box is on a wall, the same will apply — so choose a spot that is shaded by a tree or a climbing plant. Keep the box level or tilted slightly down so that the hole is not exposed to rain. Avoid trees that cats like to climb, or put on an anti-cat barrier at the bottom: an inverted wire cone fixed to the tree about one metre above the ground usually suffices. There is nothing more upsetting than having the family cat bring you a present of the young birds that you have been watching.

Try to put the nest box in a position that looks as natural as possible and emulates a natural cavity. For your own pleasure, situate it where you can see what is going on from some convenient vantage point.

Nest box placement.

124

A BIRD GARDEN

Food, shelter and water are the necessities for all birds at all seasons. A simple bird feeder will bring a variety of seed-eating birds to the garden, but there is little chance of luring insect-eating birds without an appealing environment for them. Even some of the seed-eating species are very shy at the feeder and to attract these birds it is necessary to "think natural" and create some attractive mini-habitats.

It is possible to determine the types of birds that will come to your garden by providing the sort of surroundings that give them shelter, nesting opportunities and food. Flycatchers and other insect-eating birds will be attracted in spring and summer to flower gardens where insects are likely to be abundant. Seed-eating birds will find both shelter and food in the wilder sections of a back yard, where shrubs and weeds combine to provide dense cover and year-round access to food in the form of seeds. A varied garden plot will lure birds where a flawless lawn will not, and a mix of shrubs and taller trees will attract a far greater variety and abundance of birds than a hedge of uniform trees or shrubs. It is not only berry bushes and fruit trees that provide food; seeds, insects feeding on plants, and water are at least as likely to entice birds.

Birds are also attracted to gardens where there is plenty of shelter in which to rest during the day, or to roost at night, where they can escape from the hottest weather in the summer, and find some protection in the winter. Gardens with mature trees and plenty of shrub cover will be attractive. Some birds also appreciate an area of longer grass and if it is possible to keep an area of the garden as "wild" as you can, it will attract all sorts of creatures, not just birds.

Planting to Attract Birds

Trees and Bushes An adequate food and cover supply are prerequisites for the attraction of wildlife. To achieve optimum habitat for your property, trees, shrubs and plants of diverse characteristics should be planted. Tall trees, such as most oaks or maples, provide an upper storey canopy for birds like Red-eyed Vireos and Northern Orioles. The existence of this habitat is most often limited to long-established districts within a city, or large semi-rural estate lots. It may not be practical for the average subdivision home owner to consider planting these species because the average lot is too small to accommodate them.

Sapsucker drilling holes for sap.

On the other hand, diversified habitat may be achieved by the selection of plantings that will provide ground cover or low shrubbery for species that prefer habitat either close to or on the ground. Song Sparrows and Rufous-sided Towhees are examples.

Shrubs and trees of medium height will attract still other species. The more habitat variety you can provide, the greater are your chances of attracting a variety of birds.

As with habitat, distinct preferences are exhibited by birds in their food requirements. Some species prefer soft berries while others are attracted to flower seeds or to seeds from conifer cones. Many other species are insectivorous and feed on the insects that abound on the shrubbery or the bark of trees. Young nestlings of all species are fed the soft insect larvae that are found about the leaves.

Evergreens are indispensable in a properly balanced planting program because they provide shelter and food, and interesting dark background for shrubs and flowers. On large lots they can be planted in clumps of three to five trees, two metres apart, or in double rows to form wildlife travel lanes along the edge of the property. A single evergreen planted on a small lot and surrounded by shrubs can provide some protection. Suitable species include white cedar, white spruce, and if your lot is large enough, eastern hemlock and white pine.

In addition to conifers, seed-eating birds find alders and birches attractive. The cones provide an abundance of seed that is eagerly sought by such winter birds as Common Redpolls and Pine Siskins.

The winged seeds of the Manitoba maple are particular favourites of Evening Grosbeaks. This tree is exceptionally fast growing and can provide food, shade and cover in a relatively short period of time. The rapid growth can be a disadvantage, however, to the small lot owner, as the tree can soon crowd out other desirable species.

Acorns rate close to the top of any wildlife food list because they are a staple in the diet of a large number of wildlife species, particularly during the critical winter season. Blue Jays, woodpeckers and squirrels are especially partial to oak trees.

The European mountain ash is a highly attractive ornamental tree. The ripe fruit is avidly eaten by Robins, Cedar Waxwings and other birds. Should the fruit not be eaten in the fall, it will persist throughout the winter, adding a touch of bright colour to the yard and providing a ready food supply for groups of wandering songbirds like waxwings.

Native hawthorns should not be overlooked in any backyard planting, for they possess colourful blossoms in the spring and fruit that can persist throughout the winter. The protective thorns

Starling resting on a fence post.

make the tree excellent cover for shelter and breeding. Autumn olive is a versatile shrub that can reach as high as five metres when fully grown. It offers suitable nesting habitat for many songbirds, and as a plant barrier attracts rabbits and pheasants to the shelter of its spreading branches. The berries ripen in clusters and persist on the branches throughout the winter.

The native viburnums, dogwoods and honeysuckles are useful shrubs because they provide a desirable landscape effect and adequate sites for shelter, nesting, and a reliable food supply. The native high-bush cranberry has brilliant scarlet-coloured autumn foliage and bright red berries that cling to the branches over winter. Although normally unpalatable to birds, the berries provide an emergency food supply. Nannyberry, one of the taller viburnums, reaches a height of between seven and nine metres. Persisting until late fall and early winter, the blue-black fruit is attractive to the Brown Thrasher as well as other species.

Fruits of most native dogwoods ripen in late summer or early fall, so provide little in the way of winter food. The woody branches of the red-osier dogwood, however, present a pleasing contrast against the winter snow.

Honeysuckles are often grown for their flowers and are attractive to Ruby-throated Hummingbirds. Elderberries provide an important food source, as the dark, mature fruit is ravenously eaten by most songbirds, including thrushes and warblers. Once discovered, the fruit is eaten within a few days.

The dense foliage of wild grape offers unusually good cover for small birds. The fruit is a favourite food of many songbirds, especially Northern Flickers and Northern Cardinals, and the bark is often used in nest construction. Planted along a sunny fence, grapevines make a good visual barrier.

Ground-feeding birds such a Dark-eyed Juncos and White-throated Sparrows benefit from the provision of ample ground cover. The low, spreading evergreen junipers provide excellent cover and can be planted along the edge of the patio or at the base of specimen trees.

Flowers Patches of carefully selected flowers will provide continuous colour in the garden as well as being an important food source for birds. Some common plants that produce an abundance of seed include sunflowers, cosmos, zinnias and asters. American Goldfinches seem to be particularly fond of cosmos seed. If the seed heads are left to stand throughout the winter, Dark-eyed Juncos, Blue Jays and others could well be attracted.

A specialized flower garden can be planted to attract Ruby-throated Hummingbirds. These birds readily visit morning glories, honeysuckles, hollyhocks, and columbines.

Water Birds need water throughout the year. A bird bath that is kept unfrozen in the coldest weather will attract many birds. During the summer months, a bird bath can become a busy place. Birds like to bathe more in the summer, and bird baths can provide endless pleasure for both the birds and the birdwatcher.

Choose or build a bird bath that is not too deep (no more than 7 cm), shelves gradually and is finished in a rough texture so that it is easy for birds to grip. Birds get engrossed in drinking and bathing and when they have wet feathers, they don't fly quite so well. Therefore, if the bath is on or near ground level, make sure that it is situated well away from bushes, so that cats cannot approach the bath unseen.

You can keep the water in your bird bath unfrozen during the coldest winters with a small heater available on the market, and you can make the bath particularly attractive to birds in summer by creating a trickly flow or spray of water with a small electric pump.

SEASONS OF BIRDWATCHING

Spring

The first sign of spring is often the increase in the number of ducks on the rivers and lakes, as birds from the south push north, waiting for the break-up of the ice on their inland breeding sites. Ducks begin to arrive in large numbers, many having spent the winter on the U. S. Atlantic Coast. Also arriving in early spring are Tree Swallows, Red-winged Blackbirds and Eastern Phoebes.

This is the time of year when bird-song also begins and many birds that have overwintered suddenly become more noticeable as they begin to establish breeding territories. Some species, such as Great Horned Owl, which are here throughout the year, are best found at this time of the year. Take a walk through one of the forested parks or ravines around the city at dusk or before dawn and you may well be rewarded by hearing it.

The increase in bird activity is the prelude to the breeding season and you will notice that many of the birds are actively involved in courtship behaviour. Waterfowl go through many of their breeding displays on the water, and some are very attractive to watch, particularly those of the Common Goldeneyes and Bufflehead. Like the Mallard, the Bufflehead's courtship is far from sedate, with the female frequently being pursued none too gallantly by many males.

Spring is also the time of year when it is easiest to see birds in and around the city. Not only are the numbers and variety of birds swelled by the migrants that are arriving to breed, or passing through on their way to their northern breeding grounds, but the lack of leaves on the deciduous trees makes seeing them much easier. Without doubt, early May is the best time of year to watch for warblers. Your back yard or local park may be alive with brightly coloured birds one morning but quiet the next, as the birds continue their migratory journey. Later in the year, not only will it be harder to spot them, but the young "look-alike" birds will confuse even the most experienced birder.

The display of a male Red-winged Blackbird during the mating season.

Summer

Late spring and summer is the breeding season for most birds and this means a great deal of singing, displaying and nest-building. Once the serious business of incubating the eggs and feeding the young starts, birds become less noticeable and once more secretive. It can be an advantage for a bird to announce its presence when trying to attract a mate or establish a territory, but once eggs are laid and the young hatch, there is a greater need to incubate and feed young birds, and remain undetected by predators.

For those who have put up nest boxes or have the good fortune to have their trees or gardens selected as nesting sites, this time can be great fun. There is something enormously satisfying about witnessing the breeding cycle of birds. From start to finish, it may take a chickadee only about a month to find a mate, build a nest, lay eggs, hatch them and feed the young to the point of fledging. If they happen to use a nest box that you have put up for them, this becomes a very personal experience and the sense of thrill when the young birds fly comes as quite a surprise.

Ducks moult at this time of year and both the male and the females look very much alike for a while. When ducks are moulting, it is known as the "eclipse" plumage; some species can look very different and even the common male Mallard may require more than one look before identification is possible. Birds moult at this time of year to renew their flight feathers before their fall migration, while there is still an abundance of summer food available.

Autumn

As early as August, birds that have completed their breeding cycle for the year will begin to start their migration south. Birds that breed in the Arctic must complete their breeding as quickly as possible because, by late summer, food sources are already less abundant and colder weather has begun. As young birds fledge, the birds leave their breeding grounds and begin to arrive along our shorelines. Watch for the increase in numbers of shorebirds

and waterfowl now. Rivers, bays and lakes with muddy shores and marshes are particularly good places to visit at this time of year.

Autumn is also the time of year when warblers and many of the other small birds can be frustratingly hard to identify, as the young birds and the moulting adults do not always look the way they ought to according to the books!

Swallows begin to flock in large numbers and by Labour Day, many have departed. We become aware that our summer residents have become scarce but many migrants from the north catch our attention.

Autumn is the best time to watch out for rarer birds, so be prepared to take a close look at anything that seems odd or unusual. Migrants, especially juveniles, can easily take the wrong turn. Check every bird in a flock of ducks or shorebirds and look for colours or features that are different from the majority's. Then check your field guide to see if you have found a rarity. If you think you have, call the museum or the Federation of Ontario Naturalists.

Winter

Here on the lower Great Lakes, we can look forward to many more species of birds remaining throughout the winter months than is possible in some other parts of Canada. The variety of waterfowl during the winter can be a source of many hours of fruitful birdwatching. Many bird species overwinter in this southern area — the winter temperatures are relatively warm, the lake seldom freezes, and there is little snow. This means that certain birds do not need to fly south to find a suitable place to overwinter. Scour the waterfront for diving ducks, especially for the Oldsquaw, a duck that breeds in the Arctic.

Early winter is the time of year when feeders work particularly well in attracting birds into the garden. Once you have attracted a few, more will tend to show up and linger on — perhaps even through the winter — because there is safety in numbers. Many birds react swiftly to the danger signals of other species. Although most of the smaller birds will have migrated south, some of the woodland species can be easier to see at this time of year, as there are fewer leaves on the deciduous trees and bushes. Look out for Downy and Hairy Woodpeckers, which always seem more visible in the winter, as well as winter visitors like Evening Grosbeaks.

This is a good time of year to check your nest boxes, to ensure that they are not broken and to clean them.

KEEPING BIRD NOTES

Now that you have birds coming to the feeder and birds nesting in the bird boxes, why not keep a record of which birds you see in your yard, how many of them there are, and how often you see them? Keeping records is the only way of noting changes and will provide you with many hours of pleasure. A daily or weekly checklist of sightings will tell you a great deal about your avian visitors. It will furnish a record of how numbers change throughout the seasons and from year to year, and of specific migration times of many species. You will soon know just when to expect your first Ruby-throated Hummingbird of the spring, or the first Dark-eyed Junco of the autumn. The FON's bird checklist, which you can find at the back of this book, may be especially helpful to you. It shows the geographic distribution of many Ontarian birds, their breeding status, and their relative occurrence; if you spot a

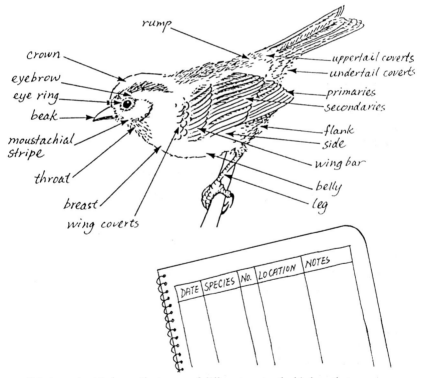

It is important to know the names of different parts of a bird, so that you can jot down specific information in your bird log.

bird which is uncommon to your area, or out of its normal range (extralimital), it would be a good idea to record it and report it to the FON. You can get additional copies of this checklist from the FON at minimal cost.

If you spend time hiking through nearby natural areas or parks, your observations will help you to remember what you saw and when. These observations will tell you what birds were common in which years and what parts of the area were particularly good for various species. As well as being of interest to you, you may be able to make an important contribution to local knowledge by helping ornithologists understand how numbers of birds in your area are changing. This sort of information is often not available when it is needed, and may also help to protect your favorite birding spot, should it be threatened with development. You could even take part in one of the many Christmas Bird Counts held in the province during the holidays; similar counts are taken of wintering birds all over North America. (You can get a list of coordinators' names from the FON.)

Keeping good records may allow you to convince the experts that you have seen a particularly rare bird, or may help you describe a problem species to an expert. Try to record a clear image of what the bird looked like — a simple line sketch is fine, although a photograph of the bird is often required for confirmation of a sighting. Include as much information as you can about the bird, its plumage characteristics, its bill, leg colour, sounds, and what behaviour the bird exhibited.

You might also want to keep a bird log. This would include the species you saw, how many, where and when (see diagram).

Keep your records in a notebook to avoid losing them. If you intend to take your notebook on hikes, choose one that has a soft waterproof cover; this will allow you to stuff it into a pocket or your pack and it will not disintegrate in the rain. A useful tip: pencils are easier than pens to sketch with, and they write more easily on damp paper.

Another good way to learn more about birds is to join your local natural history or bird society. You will meet many knowledge-able people who will be pleased to teach you what they know about birds and the best places to see them in various areas. Many organizations run field trips to some of the good birdwatching spots and provide the benefit of an expert to help with identifica-tion problems.

Good birding!

FEDERATION OF ONTARIO NATURALISTS
AND ONTARIO FIELD ORNITHOLOGISTS

Field Checklist of Birds
(1988)

This list comprises all of the bird species (437) which have been recorded in the Province of Ontario, on the basis of specimens, photographs, recordings or documented sight records accepted by the Ontario Bird Records Committee (OBRC).

The list appeared with scientific names in Ontario Birds V2, No. 1 (1984). Classification and Nomenclature follow the A.O.U. Check-List of North American Birds (6th ed. 1984), and its Supplements.

LOCALITY			
TIME/DATE			
MONTH			
YEAR			
OBSERVER			

LEGEND

Ontario is divided into north and south regions at approximately 47°N.

N - Species recorded in North; [N] indicates the OBRC requests documentation when the species is recorded in the region.
S - Species recorded in South; [S] indicates the OBRC requests documentation when the species is recorded in the region.
* - Breeding species

LOONS & GREBES
*Red-throated Loon N/S
*Pacific Loon N/[S]
*Common Loon N/S
Yellow-billed Loon [S]
*Pied-billed Grebe N/S
*Horned Grebe N/S
*Red-necked Grebe N/S
Eared Grebe [N]/S
Western Grebe [N]/[S]

TUBE NOSES
Northern Fulmar [N]/[S]
Black-capped Petrel [S]
Audubon's Shearwater [S]
Wilson's Storm-Petrel [S]
Leach's Storm-Petrel [N]/[S]
Band-rumped Storm-Petrel [S]

GANNETS, PELICANS & CORMORANTS

Northern Gannet [N]/[S]
*American White Pelican N/[S]
Brown Pelican [S]
Great Cormorant [S]
*Double-crested Cormorant N/S
Anhinga [S]

HERONS, STORKS & IBISES

*American Bittern N/S
*Least Bittern [N]/S
*Great Blue Heron N/S
*Great Egret [N]/S
*Snowy Egret [N]/S
Little Blue Heron [N]/[S]
Tricolored Heron [N]/[S]
*Cattle Egret [N]/S
*Green-backed Heron [N]/S
*Black-crowned Night-Heron [N]/S
Yellow-crowned Night-Heron [S]
White Ibis [S]
Glossy Ibis [S]
Wood Stork [S]

SWANS, GEESE & DUCKS

Fulvous Whistling-Duck [S]
*Tundra Swan [S]
Trumpeter Swan [S]
*Mute Swan [N]/S
Greater White-fronted Goose N/[S]
*Snow Goose N/S
*Ross' Goose N
Brant N/S
*Canada Goose N/S
*Wood Duck N/S
*Green-winged Teal N/S
*American Black Duck N/S
*Mallard N/S
*Northern Pintail N/S
*Blue-winged Teal N/S
*Cinnamon Teal [N]/[S]
*Northern Shoveler N/S

*Gadwall N/S
Eurasian Wigeon [N]/[S]
*American Wigeon N/S
*Canvasback N/S
*Redhead N/S
*Ring-necked Duck N/S
Tufted Duck [S]
*Greater Scaup N/S
*Lesser Scaup N/S
*Common Eider N/[S]
*King Eider N/S
Harlequin Duck [N]/S
*Oldsquaw N/S
Black Scoter N/S
*Surf Scoter N/S
*White-winged Scoter N/S
*Common Goldeneye N/S
Barrow's Goldeneye [N]/S
*Bufflehead N/S
Smew [S]
*Hooded Merganser N/S
*Common Merganser N/S
*Red-breasted Merganser N/S
*Ruddy Duck N/S

VULTURES, HAWKS, EAGLES & FALCONS

Black Vulture [S]
*Turkey Vulture N/S
*Osprey N/S
American Swallow-tailed Kite [N]/[S]
Mississippi Kite [S]
*Bald Eagle N/S
*Northern Harrier N/S
*Sharp-shinned Hawk N/S
*Cooper's Hawk N/S
*Northern Goshawk N/S
*Red-shouldered Hawk N/S
*Broad-winged Hawk N/S
Swainson's Hawk [N]/[S]
*Red-tailed Hawk N/S
*Rough-legged Hawk N/S
*Golden Eagle N/S
Crested Caracara [N]
*American Kestrel N/S
*Merlin N/S
*Peregrine Falcon N/S
Gyrfalcon N/[S]

GROUSE & TURKEYS

* *Gray Partridge N/S
* *Ring-necked Pheasant N/S
* *Spruce Grouse N/S
* *Willow Ptarmigan N/[S]
* Rock Ptarmigan N
* *Ruffed Grouse N/S
* *Greater Prairie-Chicken [N]/[S]
* *Sharp-tailed Grouse N/S
* *Wild Turkey S
* *Northern Bobwhite S

RAILS & CRANES

* *Yellow Rail N/S
* *King Rail S
* *Virginia Rail N/S
* *Sora N/S
* Purple Gallinule [N]/[S]
* *Common Moorhen [N]/S
* *American Coot N/S
* *Sandhill Crane N/S
* Whooping Crane [S]

SHOREBIRDS

* Black-bellied Plover N/S
* *Lesser Golden-Plover N/S
* Mongolian Plover [S]
* Snowy Plover [S]
* *Semipalmated Plover N/S
* *Piping Plover N/[S]
* *Killdeer N/S
* American Oystercatcher [S]
* Black-necked Stilt [N]/[S]
* *American Avocet [N]/[S]
* *Greater Yellowlegs N/S
* *Lesser Yellowlegs N/S
* Spotted Redshank [S]
* *Solitary Sandpiper N/S
* Willet [N]/S
* Wandering Tattler [S]
* *Spotted Sandpiper N/S
* *Upland Sandpiper N/S
* Eskimo Curlew [N]/[S]
* *Whimbrel N/S
* Slender-billed Curlew [S]
* Long-billed Curlew [S]
* *Hudsonian Godwit N/S
* *Marbled Godwit N/S
* Ruddy Turnstone N/S

Red Knot N/S
Sanderling N/S
* *Semipalmated Sandpiper N/S
Western Sandpiper [N]/S
Little Stint [N]
* *Least Sandpiper N/S
White-rumped Sandpiper N/S
Baird's Sandpiper N/S
* *Pectoral Sandpiper N/S
Sharp-tailed Sandpiper [S]
Purple Sandpiper N/S
* *Dunlin N/S
Curlew Sandpiper [N]/[S]
* *Stilt Sandpiper N/S
Buff-breasted Sandpiper N/S
Ruff [N]/S
* *Short-billed Dowitcher N/S
Long-billed Dowitcher [N]/S
* *Common Snipe N/S
* *American Woodcock N/S
* *Wilson's Phalarope N/S
* *Red-necked Phalarope N/S
Red Phalarope N/S

JAEGERS, GULLS, TERNS & SKIMMERS

Pomarine Jaeger [N]/[S]
* *Parasitic Jaeger N/S
Long-tailed Jaeger N/[S]
Laughing Gull [N]/S
Franklin's Gull N/S
* *Little Gull N/S
Common Black-headed Gull [N]/S
* *Bonaparte's Gull N/S
Mew Gull [S]
* *Ring-billed Gull N/S
* *California Gull [S]
* *Herring Gull N/S
Thayer's Gull N/S
Iceland Gull N/S
Lesser Black-backed Gull [N]/S
Glaucous Gull N/S
* *Great Black-backed Gull N/S

Black-legged
 Kittiwake [N]/S
Ross' Gull [N]
Sabine's Gull N/S
Ivory Gull [N]/[S]
*Caspian Tern N/S
Royal Tern [S]
Sandwich Tern [S]
*Common Tern N/S
*Arctic Tern N/S
*Forster's Tern N/S
Least Tern [S]
Sooty Tern [S]
*Black Tern N/S
Black Skimmer [N]/[S]

ALCIDS

Dovekie [S]
Thick-billed Murre [S]
Razorbill [S]
*Black Guillemot N/[S]
Ancient Murrelet [S]
Atlantic Puffin [S]

PIGEONS & DOVES

*Rock Dove N/S
Band-tailed Pigeon [N]/[S]
White-winged Dove [N]/[S]
*Mourning Dove N/S
*Passenger Pigeon-Extinct
Common Ground Dove [N]

CUCKOOS & ANIS

*Black-billed Cuckoo N/S
*Yellow-billed Cuckoo N/S
Groove-billed Ani [N]/[S]

OWLS

*Common Barn-Owl [N]/S
*Eastern Screech-Owl [N]/S
*Great Horned Owl N/S
Snowy Owl N/S
*Northern Hawk-Owl N/S
Burrowing Owl [N]/[S]
*Barred Owl N/S
*Great Gray Owl N/S
*Long-eared Owl N/S
*Short-eared Owl N/S
*Boreal Owl N/S
*Northern Saw-whet Owl
 N/S

GOATSUCKERS

Lesser Nighthawk [S]
*Common Nighthawk N/S
Common Poorwill [N]
*Chuck-will's-widow S
*Whip-poor-will N/S

SWIFTS & HUMMINGBIRDS

*Chimney Swift N/S
*Ruby-throated
 Hummingbird N/S
Rufous Hummingbird
 [N]/[S]

KINGFISHERS

*Belted Kingfisher N/S

WOODPECKERS

Lewis' Woodpecker [S]
*Red-headed
 Woodpecker N/S
*Red-bellied
 Woodpecker [N]/S
*Yellow-bellied
 Sapsucker N/S
*Downy Woodpecker N/S
*Hairy Woodpecker N/S
*Three-toed
 Woodpecker N/S
*Black-backed
 Woodpecker N/S
*Northern Flicker N/S
*Pileated
 Woodpecker N/S

TYRANT FLYCATCHERS

*Olive-sided
 Flycatcher N/S
Western
 Wood-Pewee [N]
*Eastern
 Wood-Pewee N/S
*Yellow-bellied
 Flycatcher N/S
*Acadian Flycatcher S
*Alder Flycatcher N/S
*Willow Flycatcher [N]/S
*Least Flycatcher N/S
Gray Flycatcher [S]

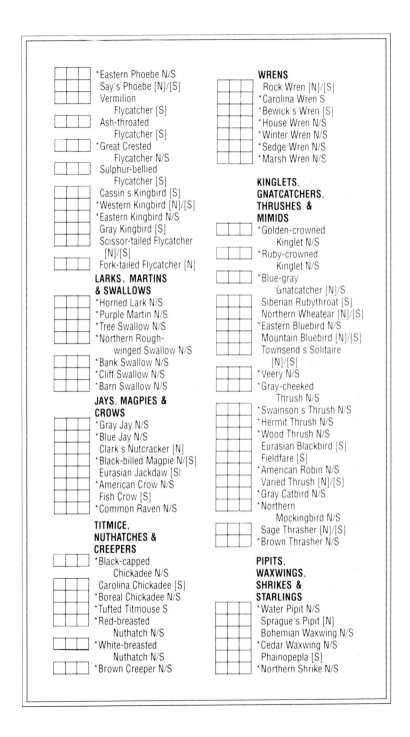

*Eastern Phoebe N/S
Say's Phoebe [N]/[S]
Vermilion
Flycatcher [S]
Ash-throated
Flycatcher [S]
*Great Crested
Flycatcher N/S
Sulphur-bellied
Flycatcher [S]
Cassin's Kingbird [S]
*Western Kingbird [N]/[S]
*Eastern Kingbird N/S
Gray Kingbird [S]
Scissor-tailed Flycatcher
[N]/[S]
Fork-tailed Flycatcher [N]

**LARKS, MARTINS
& SWALLOWS**
*Horned Lark N/S
*Purple Martin N/S
*Tree Swallow N/S
*Northern Rough-
winged Swallow N/S
*Bank Swallow N/S
*Cliff Swallow N/S
*Barn Swallow N/S

**JAYS, MAGPIES &
CROWS**
*Gray Jay N/S
*Blue Jay N/S
Clark's Nutcracker [N]
*Black-billed Magpie N/[S]
Eurasian Jackdaw [S]
*American Crow N/S
Fish Crow [S]
*Common Raven N/S

**TITMICE,
NUTHATCHES &
CREEPERS**
*Black-capped
Chickadee N/S
Carolina Chickadee [S]
*Boreal Chickadee N/S
*Tufted Titmouse S
*Red-breasted
Nuthatch N/S
*White-breasted
Nuthatch N/S
*Brown Creeper N/S

WRENS
Rock Wren [N]/[S]
*Carolina Wren S
*Bewick's Wren [S]
*House Wren N/S
*Winter Wren N/S
*Sedge Wren N/S
*Marsh Wren N/S

**KINGLETS,
GNATCATCHERS,
THRUSHES &
MIMIDS**
*Golden-crowned
Kinglet N/S
*Ruby-crowned
Kinglet N/S
*Blue-gray
Gnatcatcher [N]/S
Siberian Rubythroat [S]
Northern Wheatear [N]/[S]
*Eastern Bluebird N/S
Mountain Bluebird [N]/[S]
Townsend's Solitaire
[N]/[S]
*Veery N/S
*Gray-cheeked
Thrush N/S
*Swainson's Thrush N/S
*Hermit Thrush N/S
*Wood Thrush N/S
Eurasian Blackbird [S]
Fieldfare [S]
*American Robin N/S
Varied Thrush [N]/[S]
*Gray Catbird N/S
*Northern
Mockingbird N/S
Sage Thrasher [N]/[S]
*Brown Thrasher N/S

**PIPITS,
WAXWINGS,
SHRIKES &
STARLINGS**
*Water Pipit N/S
Sprague's Pipit [N]
Bohemian Waxwing N/S
*Cedar Waxwing N/S
Phainopepla [S]
*Northern Shrike N/S

☐ *Loggerhead Shrike [N]/S
☐ *European Starling N/S

VIREOS
☐ *White-eyed Vireo [N]/S
☐ Bell's Vireo [S]
☐ *Solitary Vireo N/S
☐ *Yellow-throated Vireo N/S
☐ *Warbling Vireo N/S
☐ *Philadelphia Vireo N/S
☐ *Red-eyed Vireo N/S

WOOD WARBLERS
☐ *Blue-winged Warbler [N]/S
☐ *Golden-winged Warbler N/S
☐ *Tennessee Warbler N/S
☐ *Orange-crowned Warbler N/S
☐ *Nashville Warbler N/S
☐ Virginia's Warbler [S]
☐ *Northern Parula N/S
☐ *Yellow Warbler N/S
☐ *Chestnut-sided Warbler N/S
☐ *Magnolia Warbler N/S
☐ *Cape May Warbler N/S
☐ *Black-throated Blue Warbler N/S
☐ *Yellow-rumped Warbler N/S
☐ Black-throated Gray Warbler [S]
☐ Townsend's Warbler [S]
☐ Hermit Warbler [S]
☐ *Black-throated Green Warbler N/S
☐ *Blackburnian Warbler N/S
☐ Yellow-throated Warbler [N]/[S]
☐ *Pine Warbler N/S
☐ *Kirtland's Warbler [S]
☐ *Prairie Warbler S
☐ *Palm Warbler N/S
☐ *Bay-breasted Warbler N/S
☐ *Blackpoll Warbler N/S

☐ *Cerulean Warbler S
☐ *Black-and-white Warbler N/S
☐ *American Redstart N/S
☐ *Prothonotary Warbler [N]/S
☐ Worm-eating Warbler S
☐ Swainson's Warbler [S]
☐ *Ovenbird N/S
☐ *Northern Waterthrush N/S
☐ *Louisiana Waterthrush S
☐ Kentucky Warbler S
☐ *Connecticut Warbler N/S
☐ *Mourning Warbler N/S
☐ MacGillivray's Warbler [S]
☐ *Common Yellowthroat N/S
☐ *Hooded Warbler [N]/S
☐ *Wilson's Warbler N/S
☐ *Canada Warbler N/S
☐ Painted Redstart [S]
☐ *Yellow-breasted Chat [N]/S

TANAGERS
☐ Summer Tanager [N]/S
☐ *Scarlet Tanager N/S
☐ Western Tanager [N]/[S]

GROSBEAKS, BUNTINGS & SPARROWS
☐ *Northern Cardinal [N]/S
☐ *Rose-breasted Grosbeak N/S
☐ Black-headed Grosbeak [N]/[S]
☐ Blue Grosbeak [S]
☐ Lazuli Bunting [N]/[S]
☐ *Indigo Bunting N/S
☐ *Dickcissel [N]/S
☐ Green-tailed Towhee [S]
☐ *Rufous-sided Towhee [N]/S
☐ Bachman's Sparrow [S]

Cassin's Sparrow [N]/[S]
*American Tree
  Sparrow N/S
*Chipping Sparrow N/S
*Clay-colored
  Sparrow N/S
*Field Sparrow [N]/S
*Vesper Sparrow N/S
*Lark Sparrow [N]/[S]
Lark Bunting [N]/[S]
*Savannah Sparrow N/S
*Grasshopper
  Sparrow [N]/S
*Henslow's Sparrow S
*Le Conte's Sparrow N/S
*Sharp-tailed
  Sparrow N/S
*Fox Sparrow N/S
*Song Sparrow N/S
*Lincoln's Sparrow N/S
*Swamp Sparrow N/S
*White-throated
  Sparrow N/S
Golden-crowned
  Sparrow [N]/[S]
*White-crowned
  Sparrow N/S
*Harris' Sparrow N/[S]
*Dark-eyed Junco N/S
*Lapland Longspur N/S
*Smith's Longspur N/[S]
Chestnut-collared
  Longspur [N]/[S]
Snow Bunting N/S

**MEADOWLARKS,
BLACKBIRDS &
ORIOLES**
*Bobolink N/S
*Red-winged
  Blackbird N/S
*Eastern Meadowlark N/S
*Western
  Meadowlark N/S
*Yellow-headed
  Blackbird N/S
*Rusty Blackbird N/S
*Brewer's Blackbird N/S
Great-tailed Grackle [N]
*Common Grackle N/S

*Brown-headed
  Cowbird N/S
*Orchard Oriole [N]/S
*Northern Oriole N/S
Scott's Oriole [N]

FINCHES
Brambling [N]
Rosy Finch [N]
*Pine Grosbeak N/S
*Purple Finch N/S
*House Finch [N]/S
*Red Crossbill N/S
*White-winged
  Crossbill N/S
*Common Redpoll N/S
Hoary Redpoll N/S
*Pine Siskin N/S
Lesser Goldfinch [S]
*American Goldfinch N/S
*Evening Grosbeak N/S

WEAVER FINCHES
*House Sparrow N/S

SUGGESTED READING

Cadman, M.D., P. Eagles and F. Heilleiner. 1987. *Atlas of the Breeding Birds of Ontario*. University of Waterloo Press. Waterloo, Ontario.

Godfrey, W.E.G. 1986. *The Birds of Canada (Second Edition)*. National Museum of Natural Sciences. Ottawa, Ontario.

Goodwin, C.E. 1982. *A Bird Finding Guide to Ontario*. University of Toronto Press. Toronto, Ontario.

Goodwin, C.E. 1988. *A Birdfinding Guide to the Toronto Region (Revised Edition)*. Clive and Jay Goodwin Enterprises Ltd. Weston, Ontario. (An indispensable aid to finding the birds of Toronto and region. Highly recommended.)

Kress, S.W. 1985. *The Audubon Society Guide to Attracting Birds*. Charles Scribner's Sons. New York .New York.

Peterson, R. T. *Guide to the Birds of North America*, 2nd Ed. National Geographic. (May be difficult to find, but worth the effort.)

Terres, J.K. 1982. *The Audubon Society Encyclopedia of North American Birds*. Alfred A. Knopf, New York, N.Y.

DIRECTORY OF ORGANIZATIONS

There are a multitude of natural history organizations in Metropolitan Toronto and Ontario which cater to nature watchers, from the beginner to the keen enthusiast. Clubs are located in all points within the Toronto birding region. I suggest that you contact the Federation of Ontario Naturalists for the address of the club nearest you.

A good natural history club is Toronto Field Naturalists. This group, like others, has regular monthly meetings and field trips. The organization covers all of the Metropolitan Toronto region.

Federation of Ontario Naturalists
355 Lesmill Road
Don Mills, Ontario
M3B 2W8
Telephone: 444-8419

Canadian Nature Federation
453 Sussex Drive
Ottawa, Ontario
K1N 9Z9
(613) 238-6154

Toronto Field Naturalists
20 College Street, Suite 4
Toronto, Ontario
M5G 1K2

INDEX TO BIRDS

ABOUT THE AUTHOR

Gerald McKeating has spent many years birding in Southern Ontario. Long active in conservation issues, he spent five years as executive director of the Federation of Ontario Naturalists before moving to the Ontario Ministry of Resources where he was responsible for the nongame and endangered species programs.
Since 1979, Gerry has worked with the Canadian Wildlife Service where he is now head of habitat conservation for the Western and Northern Region in Edmonton, Alberta.

ABOUT THE ILLUSTRATORS

Lead illustrator Ewa Pluciennik, who specialize in water colour and oil painting, was born and raise in Opole, Silesia, Poland where she receive her artistic training. She has been living in Canada for nearly five years.
Contributing illustrators Kitty Ho and Donna McKinnon are freelance artists living in Alberta. Johnston lives in British Columbia.